MW00652472

Mel Bay's

Family Hymn Book

By Pamela Cooper Bye

Chords given for Guitar and Autoharp

Includes:
"There's Something About That Name"
"Because He Lives"
"How Great Is Our God"
"God Is So Good"

1 2 3 4 5 6 7 8 9 0

FOREWORD

MEL BAY'S Family Hymn Book is one of the most carefully selected collections of religious music ever published. The large selection of 161 traditional hymns, early Christian works, contemporary religious music, and special pieces was designed to be used by the entire family. All are presented with traditional harmony, and guitar or autoharp chords accompany many pieces.

This book is meant to be treasured and enjoyed by Christians of all denominations in every conceivable setting. Brief introductions to most of the songs provide fascinating historical and background information which will enhance the understanding and enjoyment of the music.

My prayer is that through the use of this book and the combination of music and text, the "generation gap" may be narrowed, the family may be strengthened, and the worship of God in all situations may be expanded for years to come.

Pamela Cooper Bye

Contents in Alphabetical Order

*These songs are in the key of Ab and consequently must be transposed for use on the autoharp.

*These songs are in the key of Ab and consequently must be transposed for use on the autoharp.

Contents by Page Order

*These songs are in the key of Ab and consequently must be transposed for use on the autoharp.

*These songs are in the key of Ab and consequently must be transposed for use on the autoharp.

God—Father, Son, and Holy Spirit

The hymns in this section give praise to the three aspects of our God—God, the Father; God, the Son; and God, the Holy Spirit. An effort has been made to use traditional hymns, spirituals, and gospel songs, since the praise of God may be accomplished by the use of any of these. The Psalms are full of references to praising God, and one of the best of these references is Psalm 100; 1&2. "Make a joyful noise unto the Lord all ye lands. Serve the Lord with gladness: Come before His presence with singing."

PRAISE TO THE LORD, THE ALMIGHTY

Joachim Neander
Catherine Winkworth, tr.

Straslund Gesangbuch

HYMN TUNE: LOBE DEN HERREN

Serve the Lord with gladness: come before his presence with singing.
Psalm 100:2

HOLY, HOLY, HOLY! LORD GOD ALMIGHTY

This great old hymn of the Church by Bishop Reginald Heber first appeared in 1826 in Selections of Psalms and Hymns for the Parish Church of Banbury. The hymn tune "Nicaea" was composed by John B. Dykes in 1861 for use with this text. The hymn tune is named after the Nicaean Council, 325 A.D., and it clearly justifies the Christian praise of the Trinity--God, the Father; God, the Son; and God, the Holy Spirit.

Reginald Heber

John B. Dykes

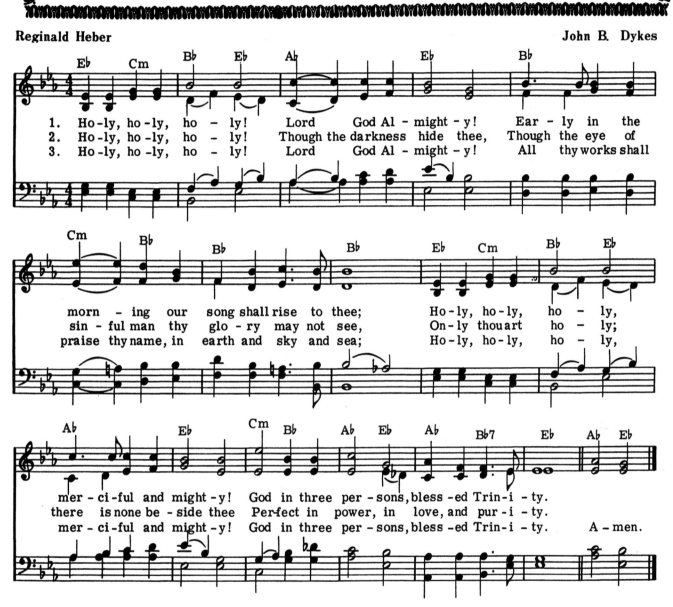

1. Ho-ly, ho-ly, ho - ly! Lord God Al - might - y! Ear - ly in the morn - ing our song shall rise to thee; Ho-ly, ho-ly, ho - ly, mer - ci-ful and might-y! God in three per-sons, bless-ed Trin-i - ty.

2. Ho-ly, ho-ly, ho - ly! Though the darkness hide thee, Though the eye of sin - ful man thy glo - ry may not see, On-ly thou art ho - ly; there is none be - side thee Per-fect in power, in love, and pur-i - ty.

3. Ho-ly, ho-ly, ho - ly! Lord God Al - might - y! All thy works shall praise thy name, in earth and sky and sea; Ho-ly, ho-ly, ho - ly, mer - ci-ful and might-y! God in three per-sons, bless-ed Trin-i - ty. A - men.

HYMN TUNE: NICAEA

It came even to pass, as the trumpeters and singers were as one, to make one sound to be heard in praising and thanking the Lord; and when they lifted up their voice with the trumpets and cymbals and instruments of music, and praised the Lord, saying, For he is good; for his mercy endureth forever: that then the house was filled with a cloud, even the house of the Lord.

II. Chronicles 5:13

PRAISE THE LORD! YE HEAVENS ADORE HIM

Stanzas 1+2, Foundling Hospital Collection
Stanza 3, Edward Osler

Rowland Prichard

1. Praise the Lord! Ye heavens, a-dore him! Praise him, an-gels in the height!
2. Praise the Lord, for he is glo-rious! Nev-er shall his prom-ise fail;
3. Wor-ship, hon-or, glo-ry, bless-ing, Lord, we of-fer un-to thee;

Sun and moon, re-joice be-fore him! Praise him, all ye stars of light!
God hath made his saints vic-to-rious; Sin and death shall not pre-vail.
Young and old, thy praise ex-press-ing, In glad hom-age bend the knee.

Praise the Lord, for he hath spo-ken! Worlds his might-y voice o-beyed:
Praise the God of our sal-va-tion! Hosts on high, his power pro-claim!
All the saints in heaven a-dore thee; We would bow be-fore thy throne.

Laws which nev-er shall be bro-ken For their guid-ance he hath made.
Heaven and earth and all cre-a-tion, Laud and mag-ni-fy his name!
As thine an-gels serve be-fore thee, So on earth thy will be done. A-men.

HYMN TUNE: HYFRYDOL

Sing unto the Lord with thanksgiving; sing praise upon the harp unto our God.
Psalm 147:7

IMMORTAL, INVISIBLE, GOD ONLY WISE

This great praise hymn is based on I Timothy 1:17, "Now unto the King, eternal, immortal, invisible, the only wise God, be honor and glory forever and ever". The hymn tune "Joanna" is Welsh and was first used in the early 1800's. The merciful, diligent, loving God is exemplified by the glorious words of this majestic hymn.

Walter C. Smith   Welsh Hymn Melody

1. Im - mor-tal, in - vis - i - ble, God on - ly wise,
In light in - ac - ces - si - ble hid from our eyes,
Most bless - ed, most glo - rious, the An - cient of Days,
Al - might - y, vic - to - rious, thy great name we praise.

2. Un - rest - ing, un - hast - ing, and si - lent as light,
Nor want - ing nor wast - ing, thou rul - est in might;
Thy jus - tice like moun-tains high soar - ing a - bove
Thy clouds which are foun-tains of good-ness and love.

3. To all, life thou giv - est, to both great and small;
In all, life thou liv - est, the true life of all;
Thy wis - dom so bound - less, thy mer - cy so free,
E - ter - nal thy good-ness, for naught changeth thee.

4. Great Fa - ther of Glo - ry, pure Fa - ther of Light,
Thine an - gels a - dore thee, all veil - ing their sight;
All praise we would ren - der; O help us to see
'Tis on - ly the splen-dor of light hid - eth thee. A - men.

HYMN TUNE: JOANNA

11

THIS IS MY FATHER'S WORLD

M. D. Babcock

Franklin Sheppard

1. This is my Fa-ther's world, And to my lis-tening ears All
2. This is my Fa-ther's world: The birds their car-ols raise; The
3. This is my Fa-ther's world: O let me ne'er for-get That,

na-ture sings, and round me rings The mu-sic of the spheres.
morn-ing light, the lil-y white, De-clare their mak-er's praise.
though the wrong seems oft so strong, God is the Rul-er yet.

This is my Fa-ther's world: I rest me in the thought Of
This is my Fa-ther's world: He shines in all that's fair; In the
This is my Fa-ther's world: Why should my heart be sad? The

rocks and trees, of skies and seas; His hand the won-ders wrought.
rus-tling grass I hear him pass; He speaks to me ev-ery-where.
Lord is King; let the heav-ens ring. God reigns; let earth be glad. A - men.

HYMN TUNE: TERRA BEATA

O sing unto the Lord a new song: sing unto the Lord, all the earth.

Psalm 96:1&2

FOR THE BEAUTY OF THE EARTH

Folliott Pierpoint

Conrad Kocher

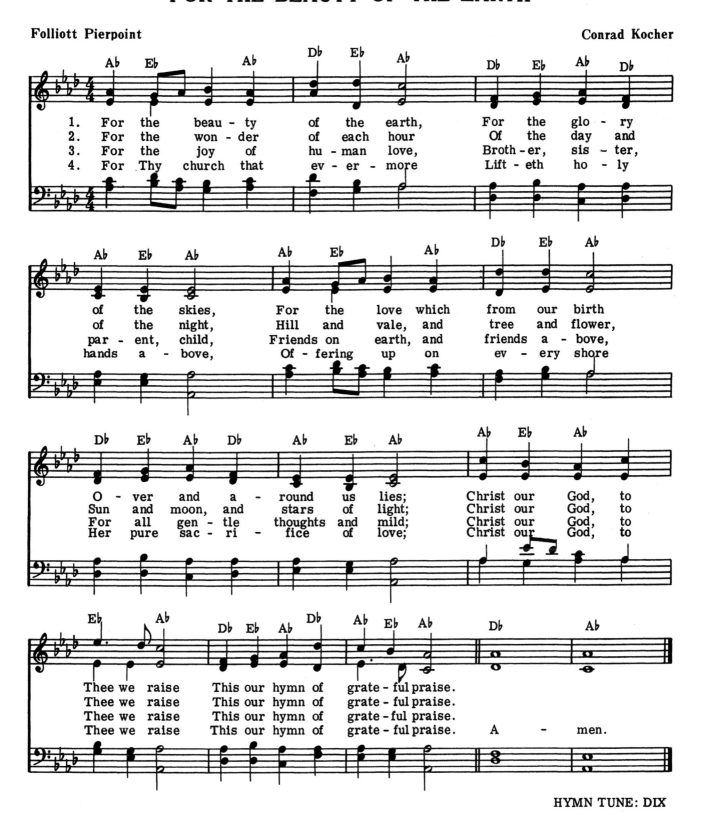

1. For the beau-ty of the earth, For the glo-ry of the skies, For the love which from our birth O-ver and a-round us lies; Christ our God, to Thee we raise This our hymn of grate-ful praise.

2. For the won-der of each hour Of the day and of the night, Hill and vale, and tree and flower, Sun and moon, and stars of light; Christ our God, to Thee we raise This our hymn of grate-ful praise.

3. For the joy of hu-man love, Broth-er, sis-ter, par-ent, child, Friends on earth, and friends a-bove, For all gen-tle thoughts and mild; Christ our God, to Thee we raise This our hymn of grate-ful praise.

4. For Thy church that ev-er-more Lift-eth ho-ly hands a-bove, Of-fering up on ev-ery shore Her pure sac-ri-fice of love; Christ our God, to Thee we raise This our hymn of grate-ful praise. A-men.

HYMN TUNE: DIX

Make a joyful noise unto the Lord, all the earth: make a loud noise, and rejoice, and sing praise. Sing unto the Lord with the harp; with the harp, and the voice of a psalm. With trumpets and sound of cornet make a joyful noise before the Lord, the King.

Psalm 98:4-6

NOW, ON LAND AND SEA DESCENDING

Samuel Longfellow

Arr. by J. A. Stevenson

HYMN TUNE: VESPER HYMN

Let the word of Christ dwell in you richly in all wisdom; teaching and admonishing one another in psalms, and hymns, and spiritual songs, singing with grace in your hearts to the Lord.

Colossians 3:16

ALL PEOPLE THAT ON EARTH DO DWELL

William Kethe

Genevan Psalter

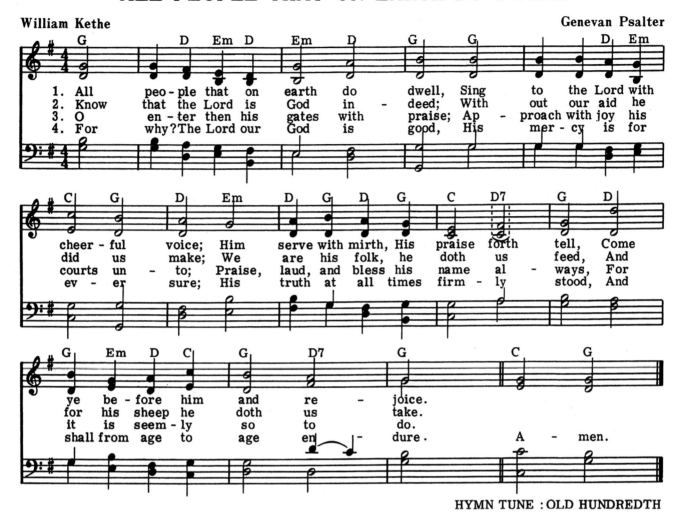

HYMN TUNE : OLD HUNDREDTH

O GOD, OUR HELP IN AGES PAST

Isaac Watts

William Croft

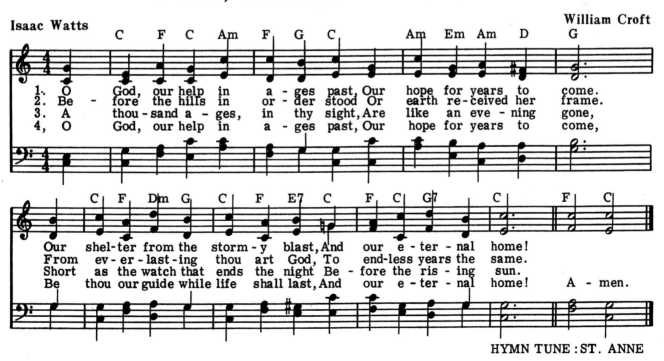

HYMN TUNE : ST. ANNE

15

A MIGHTY FORTRESS IS OUR GOD

Both the text and music of this Reformation giant were written by Martin Luther in 1529. The words are a paraphrase of Psalm 46, and this hymn stands as one of the most-sung hymns in the history of the Protestant church.

Martin Luther   Martin Luther

1. A might-y for-tress is our God, A bul-wark nev-er fail-ing;
2. Did we in our own strength con-fide, Our striv-ing would be los-ing;
3. And though this world, with dev-ils filled, Should threat-en to un-do us,
4. God's word a-bove all earth-ly powers, No thanks to them, a-bid-eth;

Our help-er he a-mid the flood Of mor-tal ills pre-vail-ing.
Were not the right Man on our side, The Man of God's own choos-ing.
We will not fear, for God has willed His truth to tri-umph through us.
The Spir-it and the gifts are ours Through him who with us sid-eth.

For still our an-cient foe Doth seek to work us woe; His craft and power are great,
Dost ask who that may be? Christ Je-sus, it is he; Lord Sa-ba-oth his name,
The prince of dark-ness grim—We trem-ble not for him; His rage we can en-dure,
Let goods and kin-dred go, This mor-tal life al-so; The bod-y they may kill:

And, armed with cru-el hate, On earth is not his e-qual.
From age to age the same, And he must win the bat-tle.
For lo! His doom is sure; One lit-tle word shall fell him.
God's truth a-bid-eth still; His king-dom is for-ev-er. A-men.

HYMN TUNE: EIN' FESTE BURG

COME, THOU ALMIGHTY KING

Whitefield's Collection

Felice de Giardini

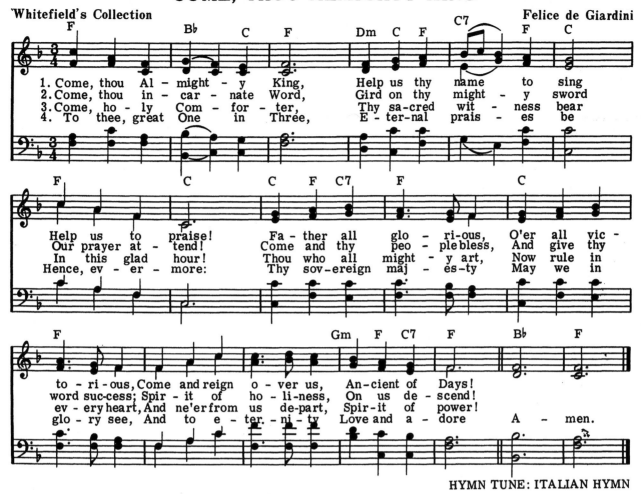

1. Come, thou Al - might - y King, Help us thy name to sing
2. Come, thou in - car - nate Word, Gird on thy might - y sword
3. Come, ho - ly Com - for - ter, Thy sa - cred wit - ness bear
4. To thee, great One in Three, E - ter - nal prais - es be

Help us to praise! Fa - ther all glo - ri-ous, O'er all vic-ti -
Our prayer at - tend! Come and thy peo - ple bless, And give thy
In this glad hour! Thou who all might - y art, Now rule in
Hence, ev - er - more: Thy sov-ereign maj - es-ty May we in

to - ri-ous, Come and reign o - ver us, An-cient of Days!
word suc-cess; Spir - it of ho - li-ness, On us de - scend!
ev - ery heart, And ne'er from us de-part, Spir-it of power!
glo - ry see, And to e - ter - ni-ty Love and a - dore A - men.

HYMN TUNE: ITALIAN HYMN

ADORE AND PRAISE THE LORD

Pamela C. Bye

William H. Walter

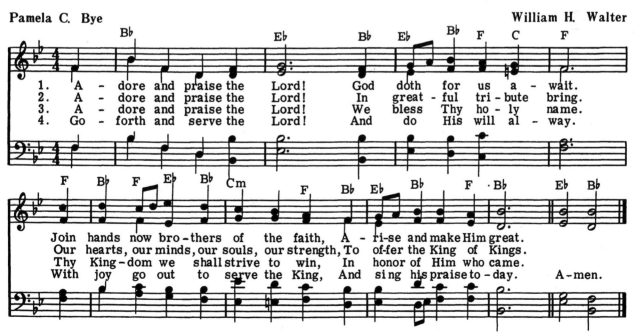

1. A - dore and praise the Lord! God doth for us a - wait.
2. A - dore and praise the Lord! In great - ful tri - bute bring.
3. A - dore and praise the Lord! We bless Thy ho - ly name.
4. Go - forth and serve the Lord! And do His will al - way.

Join hands now bro - thers of the faith, A - ri-se and make Him great.
Our hearts, our minds, our souls, our strength, To of-fer the King of Kings.
Thy King-dom we shall strive to win, In honor of Him who came.
With joy go out to serve the King, And sing his praise to - day. A-men.

HYMN TUNE: FESTAL SONG

O WORSHIP THE KING

This hymn is a paraphrase of Psalm 104, and it was first published in 1833. The hymn tune "Lyons" was written by William Gardiner, a close associate of many early nineteenth century musicians, such as Franz Joseph Haydn, upon whose melodic themes scholars think "Lyons" is based.

Robert Grant   William Gardiner

1. O worship the King, all glorious above,
O gratefully sing his power and his love;
Our Shield and Defender, the Ancient of Days,
Pavilioned in splendor, and girded with praise.

2. O tell of his might, O sing of his grace,
Whose robe is the light, whose canopy space.
His chariots of wrath the deep thunderclouds form,
And dark is his path on the wings of the storm.

3. Thy bountiful care, what tongue can recite?
It breathes in the air, it shines in the light;
It streams from the hills, it descends to the plain,
And sweetly distills in the dew and the rain.

4. Frail children of dust, and feeble as frail,
In thee do we trust, nor find thee to fail;
Thy mercies, how tender! How firm to the end!
Our Maker, Defender, Redeemer, and Friend. A-men.

* An E7 chord may be used on the autoharp in place of the E chord.   HYMN TUNE: LYONS

PRAISE, MY SOUL, THE KING OF HEAVEN

The hymn tune "Regent Square" was composed in 1867 by Henry Smart for an English Presbyterian hymnal. The text is a paraphrase of Psalm 103, and the stately words attest once again to the unchanging, merciful nature of God. Lyte closes his hymn by calling all of us to praise God repeatedly and in every situation.

Henry Lyte   Henry Smart

1. Praise, my soul, the King of heav-en, To his feet thy
2. Praise him for his grace and fa-vor To our fa-thers
3. Fa-ther-like, he tends, and spares us; Well our fee-ble
4. An-gels in the height, a-dore him; Ye be-hold him

trib-ute bring; Ran-somed, healed, re-stored, for-giv-en
in dis-tress; Praise him, still the same as ev-er,
frame he knows; In his hands he gent-ly bears us,
face to face; Saints tri-um-phant, bow be-fore him,

Ev-er-more his prais-es sing. Al-le-lu-ia!
Slow to chide, and swift to bless. Al-le-lu-ia!
Res-cues us from all our foes. Al-le-lu-ia!
Gath-ered in from ev-ery race. Al-le-lu-ia!

Al-le-lu-ia! Praise the ev-er last-ing King.
Al-le-lu-ia! Glo-rious in his faith-ful-ness.
Al-le-lu-ia! Wide-ly yet his mer-cy flows.
Al-le-lu-ia! Praise with us the God of grace. A-men.

HYMN TUNE: REGENT SQUARE

GOD OF OUR FATHERS, WHOSE ALMIGHTY HAND

The original hymn was written for the celebration of the Fourth of July, 1876, and set to the tune "Russian Hymn". George W. Warren wrote the tune "National Hymn" with which the text is now more often associated.

Daniel C. Roberts

George W. Warren

1. God of our fa - thers, whose al - might - y hand
2. Thy love di - vine hath led us in the
3. From war's a - larms, from dead - ly pes - ti -
4. Re - fresh thy peo - ple on their toil - some

hand   Leads forth in beau - ty all the star - ry band
past;   In this free land by thee our lot is cast;
lence,   Be thy strong arm our ev - er sure de - fense;
way;   Lead us from night to nev - er - end - ing day;

Of   shin - ing worlds in splen - dor through the skies,
Be   thou our ru - ler, guard - ian, guide, and stay;
Thy   true re li - gion in our hearts in - crease,
Fill all our lives with love and grace di - vine,

Our grate - ful songs be - fore thy throne a - rise.
Thy Word our law, thy paths our cho - sen way.
Thy boun - teous good - ness nour - ish us in peace.
And glo - ry, laud, and praise be ev - er thine. A - men.

* (A Bb minor chord cannot be played on the autoharp)

HYMN TUNE: NATIONAL HYMN

TO GOD BE THE GLORY

As with most gospel hymns, this hymn explains what God has done in giving his Son for our salvation, and it offers an invitation to receive those benefits purchased by Christ's blood. The third verse expresses the belief that the life with Jesus after death will be more perfect than anything which can be imagined. The hymn first appeared in <u>Brightest and Best</u> in 1875.

Fanny Crosby

William H. Doane

1. To God be the glo - ry! Great things he hath done; So loved he the world that he gave us his Son, Who yield - ed his life an a - tone-ment for sin, And o - pened the life-gate that all may go in.
2. O per - fect re-demp-tion, the pur-chase of blood, To ev - ery be - liev - er the prom-ise of God! The vil - est of - fend-er who tru - ly be-lieves, That mo-ment from Je - sus a par-don re - ceives.
3. Great things he hath taught us, great things he hath done, And great our re-joicing through Je - sus the Son! But pu - rer and higher and great-er will be Our won-der, our trans-port, when Je - sus we see.

REFRAIN

Praise the Lord! Praise the Lord! Let the earth hear his voice! Praise the Lord! Praise the Lord! Let the peo-ple re - joice! O come to the Fa-ther, through Je-sus the Son, And give him the glo-ry! Great things he hath done.

HYMN TUNE: TO GOD BE THE GLORY

21

O FOR A THOUSAND TONGUES TO SING

This is perhaps the most joyous and well-recognized of the wealth of hymns in the Christian Church. On the anniversary of his conversion, Charles Wesley is said to have recalled the words spoken by Peter Mohler, a Moravian church leader, "Had I a thousand tongues, I would praise God with them all".

Charles Wesley

Carl Glaser
Arr. by Lowell Mason

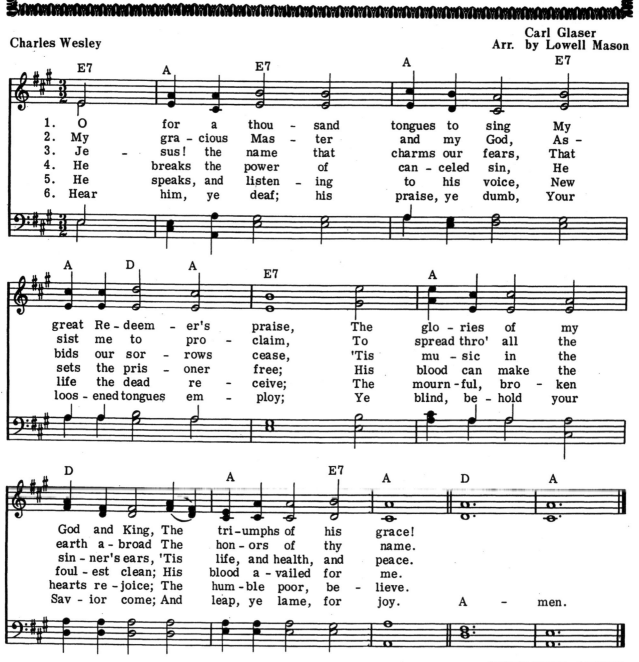

1. O for a thou - sand tongues to sing My great Re - deem - er's praise, The glo - ries of my God and King, The tri - umphs of his grace!
2. My gra - cious Mas - ter and my God, As - sist me to pro - claim, To spread thro' all the earth a - broad The hon - ors of thy name.
3. Je - sus! the name that charms our fears, That bids our sor - rows cease, 'Tis mu - sic in the sin - ner's ears, 'Tis life, and health, and peace.
4. He breaks the power of can - celed sin, He sets the pris - oner free; His blood can make the foul - est clean; His blood a - vailed for me.
5. He speaks, and listen - ing to his voice, New life the dead re - ceive; The mourn - ful, bro - ken hearts re - joice; The hum - ble poor, be - lieve.
6. Hear him, ye deaf; his praise, ye dumb, Your loos - ened tongues em - ploy; Ye blind, be - hold your Sav - ior come; And leap, ye lame, for joy. A - men.

HYMN TUNE: AZMON

Praise ye the Lord. Praise God in his sanctuary: praise him in the firmament of his power. Praise him for his mighty acts: praise him according to his excellent greatness. Praise him with the sound of the trumpet: praise him with the psaltery and harp. Praise him with the timbrel and dance; praise him with stringed instruments and organs. Praise him upon the loud cymbals: praise him upon the high-sounding cymbals. Let everything that hath breath praise the Lord. Praise ye the Lord.

Psalm 150

COME, CHRISTIANS, JOIN TO SING

One of the most exciting Protestant hymns of the early 1800's, "Come, Christians, Join to Sing", is often used as a call to worship or an entrance hymn to begin the worship service. Benjamin Carr was a well-respected American composer and music publisher who studied under Charles Wesley before coming to the United States. He was also an accomplished organist.

Christian Bateman   Benjamin Carr

1. Come, Chris-tians, join to sing   Al - le - lu - ia!   A - men!
2. Come, lift your hearts on high;   Al - le - lu - ia!   A - men!
3. Praise yet our Christ a - gain;   Al - le - lu - ia!   A - men!

Loud praise to Christ our King;   Al - le - lu - ia!   A - men!
Let prais - es fill the sky;   Al - le - lu - ia!   A - men!
Life shall not end the strain;   Al - le - lu - ia!   A - men!

Let all, with heart and voice,   Be - fore his throne re - joice;
He is our guide and friend;   To us he'll con - de - scend;
On heav-en's bliss-ful shore   His good-ness we'll a - dore,

Praise is his gra-cious choice: Al - le - lu - ia!   A - men!
His love shall nev - er end: Al - le - lu - ia!   A - men!
Sing - ing for - ev - er - more: Al - le - lu - ia!   A - men!   A - men.

HYMN TUNE: MADRID

23

WHEN MORNING GILDS THE SKIES

The theme of universal praise dominates this hymn of the Victorian Period. The original hymn text was German, and a translation was made in 1858 by Edward Caswall. The hymn tune "Laudes Domini" was by Joseph Barnby, the composer of at least 240 hymns and the editor of several hymnals for use in Sunday School and the home.

Edward Caswall, tr.   Joseph Barnby

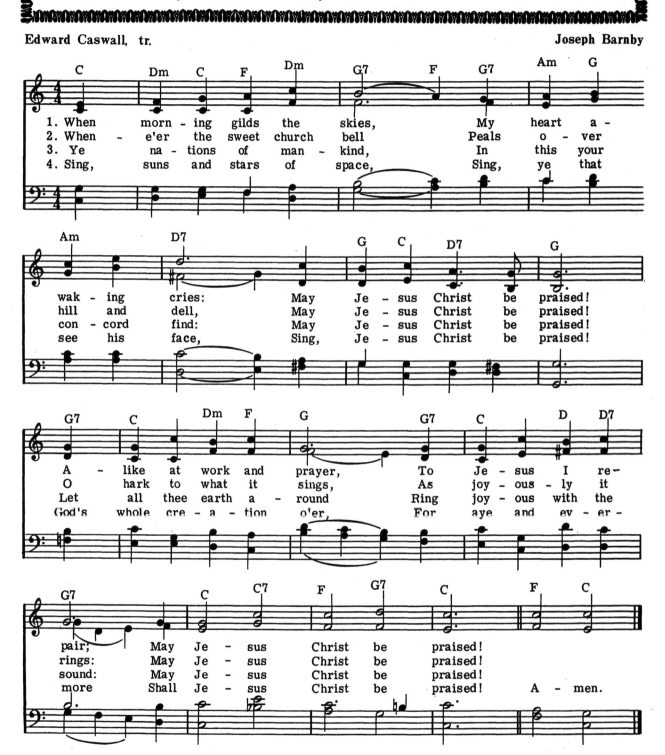

HYMN TUNE: LAUDES DOMINI

ALL HAIL THE POWER OF JESUS' NAME

The hymn tune "Coronation" was composed by Oliver Holden in 1793. The words were written by Edward Perronet, an associate of John and Charles Wesley in England, who based it on the words from Philippians 2: 9-11. Before his death, Perronet broke with the Wesleys and was a leader in the Methodist movement.

Edward Perronet

Oliver Holden

HYMN TUNE: CORONATION

.... Have an eye to God in every word you sing. Aim at pleasing him more than yourself, or any other creature. In order to do this attend strictly to the sense of what you sing, and see that your heart is not carried away with the sound, but offered to God continually; so shall your singing be such as the Lord will approve here; and reward you when he cometh in the clouds of heaven.

From John Wesley's preface to Sacred Melody, 1761

OH GOD, WE PRAISE THEE

Laud, C. M.

Wyeth's Repository of
Sacred Music, 1813

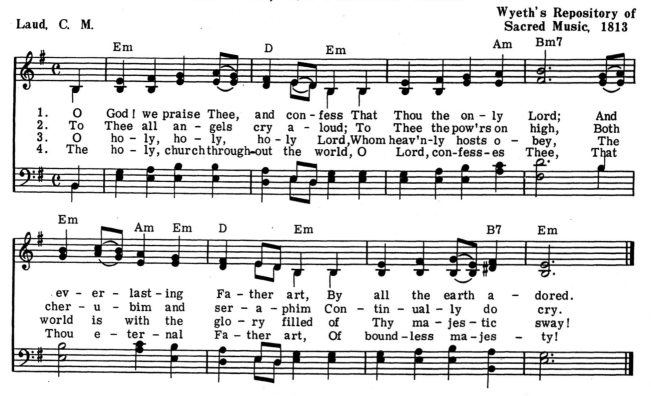

1. O God! we praise Thee, and con-fess That Thou the on-ly Lord; And
2. To Thee all an-gels cry a-loud; To Thee the pow'rs on high, Both
3. O ho-ly, ho-ly, ho-ly Lord, Whom heav'n-ly hosts o-bey, The
4. The ho-ly, church through-out the world, O Lord, con-fess-es Thee, That

ev-er-last-ing Fa-ther art, By all the earth a-dored.
cher-u-bim and ser-a-phim Con-tin-ual-ly do cry.
world is with the glo-ry filled of Thy ma-jes-tic sway!
Thou e-ter-nal Fa-ther art, Of bound-less ma-jes-ty!

PRAISE HIM IN THE MORNING

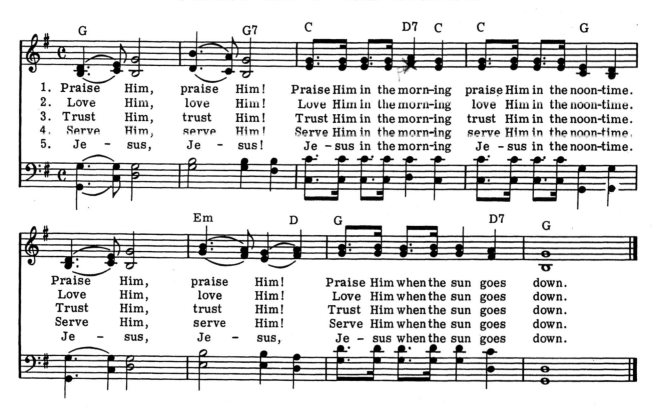

1. Praise Him, praise Him! Praise Him in the morn-ing praise Him in the noon-time.
2. Love Him, love Him! Love Him in the morn-ing love Him in the noon-time.
3. Trust Him, trust Him! Trust Him in the morn-ing trust Him in the noon-time.
4. Serve Him, serve Him! Serve Him in the morn-ing serve Him in the noon-time.
5. Je-sus, Je-sus! Je-sus in the morn-ing Je-sus in the noon-time.

Praise Him, praise Him! Praise Him when the sun goes down.
Love Him, love Him! Love Him when the sun goes down.
Trust Him, trust Him! Trust Him when the sun goes down.
Serve Him, serve Him! Serve Him when the sun goes down.
Je-sus, Je-sus, Je-sus when the sun goes down.

LET US BREAK BREAD TOGETHER

The Negro spiritual grew from the desire of the people for a better life--free of persecution, "on the other side of Jordan" with the Savior in whom they fervently believed. These songs, once sung only in slave cabins or cotton fields, have been incorporated into the worship of practically all denominations as they express with simplicity and sincerity man's basic goal of achieving the Promised Land. "Let Us Break Bread Together" is often used in the Communion service.

Traditional   Spiritual

1. Let us break bread to-geth-er on our knees, on our knees;
2. Let us drink wine to-geth-er on our knees, on our knees;
3. Let us praise God to-geth-er on our knees, on our knees;

Let us break bread to-geth-er on our knees, on our knees.
Let us drink wine to-geth-er on our knees, on our knees.
Let us praise God to-geth-er on our knees, on our knees.

When I fall on my knees, with my face to the ris-ing sun,

O Lord, have mer-cy on me. on me.

HYMN TUNE: COMMUNION SPIRITUAL

WERE YOU THERE WHEN THEY CRUCIFIED MY LORD?

This well-known Negro spiritual describes with simplicity the events surrounding the Crucifixion, and it personally involves the singer with the haunting question, "Were you there?" The spiritual was originally published in Old Plantation Hymns in 1899.

Traditional   Spiritual

1. Were you there when they cru-ci-fied my Lord? (were you there?)
2. Were you there when they nailed him to the tree? (to the tree?)
3. Were you there when they laid him in the tomb? (in the tomb?)
4. Were you there when he rose up from the tomb? (from the tomb?)

Were you there when they cru-ci-fied my Lord?
Were you there when they nailed him to the tree?
Were you there when they laid him in the tomb?
Were you there when he rose up from the tomb?

Oh! Some-times it caus-es me to trem-ble, trem-ble,
Oh! Some-times it caus-es me to trem-ble, trem-ble,
Oh! Some-times it caus-es me to trem-ble, trem-ble,
Oh! Some-times I feel like shout-ing glo-ry, glo-ry,

trem-ble! Were you there when they cru-ci-fied my Lord?
trem-ble! Were you there when they nailed him to the tree?
trem-ble! Were you there when they laid him in the tomb?
glo-ry! Were you there when he rose up from the tomb?

IN THE CROSS OF CHRIST I GLORY

The significance of the Resurrection is made abundantly clear through the words of this nineteenth century hymn. The text by John Bowring is based on Galatians 6:14, "But God forbid that I should glory, save in the cross of our Lord Jesus Christ".... The hymn tune "Rathbun" was written by Ithamar Conkey while he was the organist of Central Baptist Church is Norwich, Connecticut.

John Bowring

Ithamar Conkey

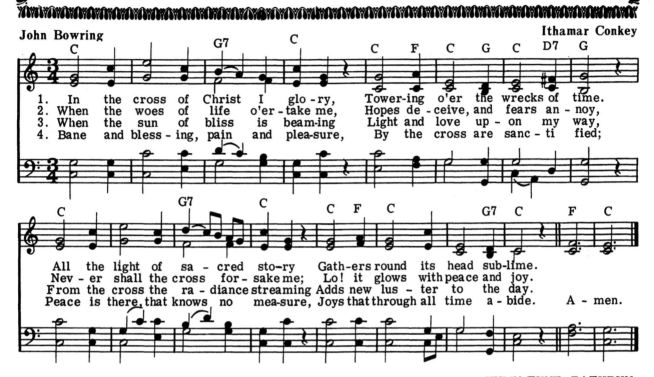

1. In the cross of Christ I glo-ry, Tow-er-ing o'er the wrecks of time.
2. When the woes of life o'er-take me, Hopes de-ceive, and fears an-noy,
3. When the sun of bliss is beam-ing Light and love up-on my way,
4. Bane and bless-ing, pain and plea-sure, By the cross are sanc-ti-fied;

All the light of sa-cred sto-ry Gath-ers round its head sub-lime.
Nev-er shall the cross for-sake me; Lo! it glows with peace and joy.
From the cross the ra-diance streaming Adds new lus-ter to the day.
Peace is there, that knows no mea-sure, Joys that through all time a-bide. A-men.

HYMN TUNE: RATHBUN

"MAN OF SORROWS," WHAT A NAME

Philip P. Bliss

Philip P. Bliss

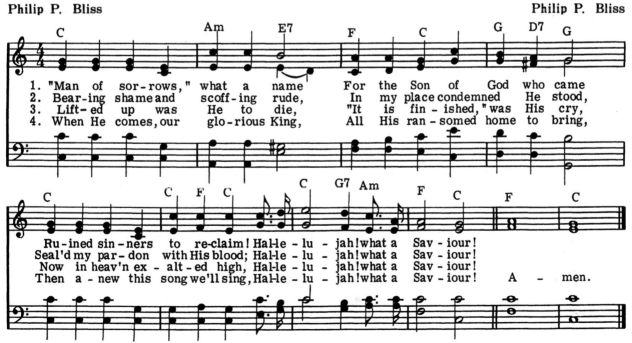

1. "Man of sor-rows," what a name For the Son of God who came
2. Bear-ing shame and scoff-ing rude, In my place condemned He stood,
3. Lift-ed up was He to die, "It is fin-ished," was His cry,
4. When He comes, our glo-rious King, All His ran-somed home to bring,

Ru-ined sin-ners to re-claim! Hal-le-lu-jah! what a Sav-iour!
Seal'd my par-don with His blood; Hal-le-lu-jah! what a Sav-iour!
Now in heav'n ex-alt-ed high, Hal-le-lu-jah! what a Sav-iour!
Then a-new this song we'll sing, Hal-le-lu-jah! what a Sav-iour! A-men.

HYMN TUNE: HALLELUJAH! WHAT A SAVIOUR

WHEN I SURVEY THE WONDROUS CROSS

Isaac Watts

Arr. by Lowell Mason

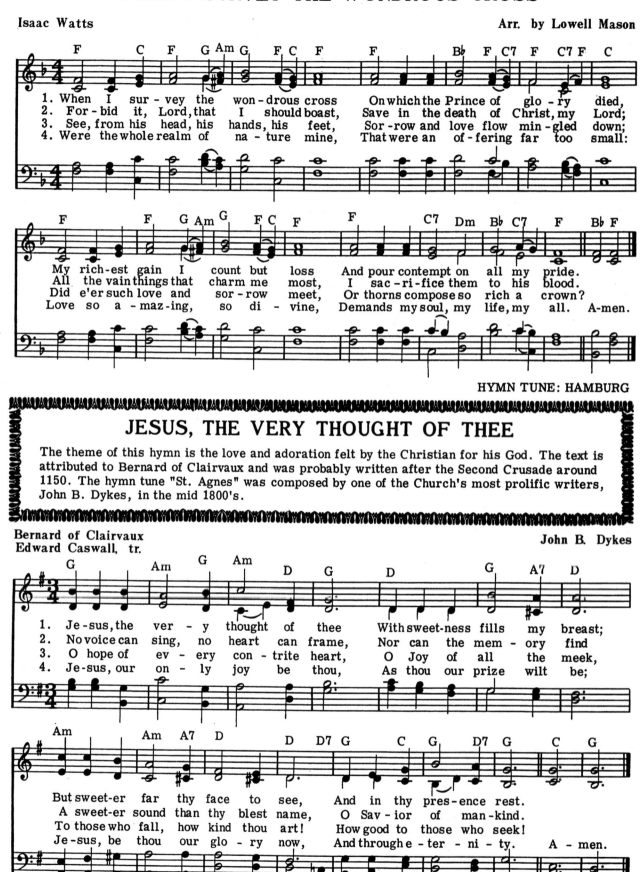

1. When I sur-vey the won-drous cross On which the Prince of glo-ry died,
2. For-bid it, Lord, that I should boast, Save in the death of Christ, my Lord;
3. See, from his head, his hands, his feet, Sor-row and love flow min-gled down;
4. Were the whole realm of na-ture mine, That were an of-fering far too small:

My rich-est gain I count but loss, And pour contempt on all my pride.
All the vain things that charm me most, I sac-ri-fice them to his blood.
Did e'er such love and sor-row meet, Or thorns compose so rich a crown?
Love so a-maz-ing, so di-vine, Demands my soul, my life, my all. A-men.

HYMN TUNE: HAMBURG

JESUS, THE VERY THOUGHT OF THEE

The theme of this hymn is the love and adoration felt by the Christian for his God. The text is attributed to Bernard of Clairvaux and was probably written after the Second Crusade around 1150. The hymn tune "St. Agnes" was composed by one of the Church's most prolific writers, John B. Dykes, in the mid 1800's.

Bernard of Clairvaux
Edward Caswall, tr.

John B. Dykes

1. Je-sus, the ver-y thought of thee With sweet-ness fills my breast;
2. No voice can sing, no heart can frame, Nor can the mem-ory find
3. O hope of ev-ery con-trite heart, O Joy of all the meek,
4. Je-sus, our on-ly joy be thou, As thou our prize wilt be;

But sweet-er far thy face to see, And in thy pres-ence rest.
A sweet-er sound than thy blest name, O Sav-ior of man-kind.
To those who fall, how kind thou art! How good to those who seek!
Je-sus, be thou our glo-ry now, And through e-ter-ni-ty. A-men.

HYMN TUNE: ST. AGNES

30

RIDE ON! RIDE ON IN MAJESTY

Henry Milman

John B. Dykes

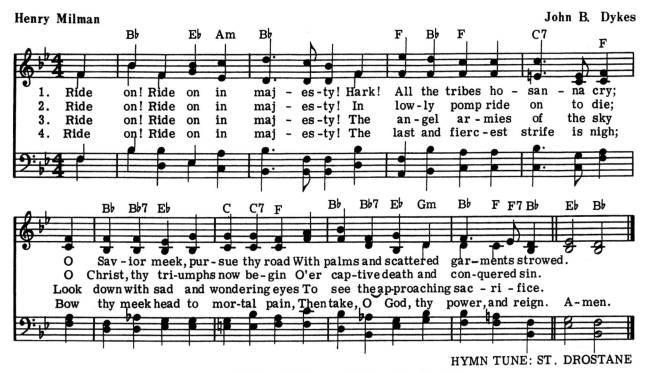

1. Ride on! Ride on in maj - es - ty! Hark! All the tribes ho - san - na cry;
2. Ride on! Ride on in maj - es - ty! In low - ly pomp ride on to die;
3. Ride on! Ride on in maj - es - ty! The an - gel ar - mies of the sky
4. Ride on! Ride on in maj - es - ty! The last and fierc - est strife is nigh;

O Sav - ior meek, pur - sue thy road With palms and scattered gar - ments strowed.
O Christ, thy tri - umphs now be - gin O'er cap - tive death and con - quered sin.
Look down with sad and wondering eyes To see the ap - proaching sac - ri - fice.
Bow thy meek head to mor - tal pain, Then take, O God, thy power, and reign. A - men.

HYMN TUNE: ST. DROSTANE

REJOICE, THE LORD IS KING

Charles Wesley

John Darwall

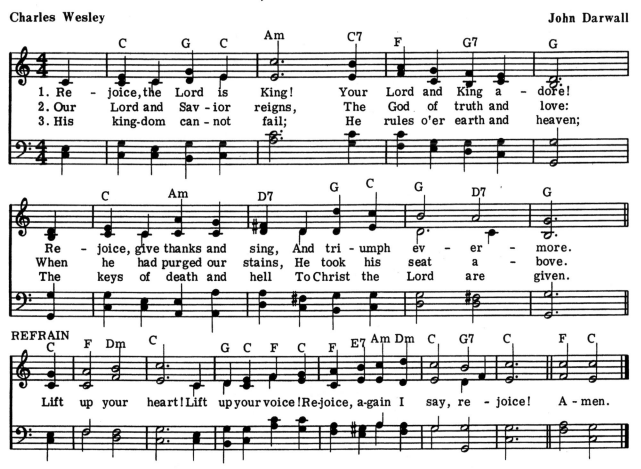

1. Re - joice, the Lord is King! Your Lord and King a - dore!
2. Our Lord and Sav - ior reigns, The God of truth and love:
3. His king - dom can - not fail; He rules o'er earth and heaven;

Re - joice, give thanks and sing, And tri - umph ev - er - more.
When he had purged our stains, He took his seat a - bove.
The keys of death and hell To Christ the Lord are given.

REFRAIN

Lift up your heart! Lift up your voice! Re - joice, a - gain I say, re - joice! A - men.

HYMN TUNE: DARWALL'S 148TH.

ALL GLORY, LAUD, AND HONOR

The hymn tune "St. Theodulph" was composed by Melchior Teschner and published in Leipzig in 1615. The words were written by Saint Theodulph of Orleans while he was imprisoned at Angers. The hymn is traditionally used on any joyous occasion, but it is particularly appropriate for Palm Sunday as it embodies the excitement felt by those who watched the arrival of Jesus in Jerusalem.

Theodulph of Orleans   Melchior Teschner

HYMN TUNE: ST. THEODULPH

REJOICE, YE PURE IN HEART

The triumphant chorus of this great hymn makes it a favorite for use in services of celebration. The text was written in May, 1865, for a choir festival, and the tune "Marion" was composed by Arthur Messiter in 1883.

Edward Plumptre   Arthur Messiter

1. Re - joice, ye pure in heart! Re - joice, give thanks and sing!
2. With voice as full and strong As o - cean's surg - ing praise,
3. Bright youth and snow-crowned age, Strong men and maid - ens fair,
4. Yes, on through life's long path, Still chant -ing as ye go;

Your fes - tal ban - ner wave on high, The cross of Christ your King!
Send forth the hymns our fa - thers loved, The psalms of an - cient days.
Raise high your free, ex - ult - ing song, God's won-drous praise de - clare!
From youth to age, by night and day, In glad - ness and in woe,

Re - joice, re - joice, Re - joice, give thanks and sing! A - men.
Re-joice, re-joice,

HYMN TUNE: MARION

Sing lustily and with a good courage. Beware of singing as if you were half dead, or half asleep; but lift up your voice with strength. Be no more afraid of your voice now, nor more ashamed of its being heard, than when you sung the songs of Satan.

From John Wesley's preface to Sacred Melody, 1761

CHRIST THE LORD IS RISEN TODAY

This glorious Easter hymn was written by Charles Wesley and first appeared in Hymns and Sacred Poems published in 1739. The Alleluia at the end of the verse is reminiscent of the early Christian greeting for Easter morn, "Alleluia, the Lord is risen!" "He is risen indeed, Alleluia!"

Charles Wesley

Lyra Davidica, 1708

1. "Christ the Lord is risen to-day," Al - - le - lu - ia!
2. Lives - a gain our glo-rious King: Al - - le - lu - ia!
3. Love's re-deem-ing work is done; Al - - le - lu - ia!
4. Soar we now where Christ hath led, Al - - le - lu - ia!

Sons of men and an-gels say. Al - - le - lu - ia!
Where, O death, is now thy sting? Al - - le - lu - ia!
Fought the fight, the bat-tle won. Al - - le - lu - ia!
Fol-lowing our ex-alt-ed Head. Al - - le - lu - ia!

Raise you joys and tri-umphs high; Al - - le - lu - ia!
Once he died, our souls to save; Al - - le - lu - ia!
Death in vain for-bids him rise; Al - - le - lu - ia!
Made like him, like him we rise, Al - - le - lu - ia!

Sing, ye heavens, and earth re-ply. Al - - le - lu - ia!
Where thy vic-to-ry, O grave? Al - - le - lu - ia!
Christ hath o-pened Par-a-dise. Al - - le - lu - ia!
Ours the cross, the grave, the skies. Al - - le - lu - ia! A - men.

HYMN TUNE: EASTER HYMN

34

THE STRIFE IS O'ER

One of the greatest of all Renaissance composers, Giovanni Pierluigi da Palestrina, wrote this hymn tune in the sixteenth century. The original text was traced to a Jesuit publication of 1695. Francis Pott made the present translation in 1861, and William Monk adapted Palestrina's tune, adding the Alleluias on his own.

Giovanni Pierluigi da Palestrina
Adapted by William Monk

Francis Pott, tr.

1. The strife is o'er, the bat — tle done;
   The vic - to - ry of life is won; The song of tri - umph has be - gun. Al - le - lu - ia!
2. The powers of death have done — their worst,
   But Christ their le - gions hath dis - persed; Let shouts of ho - ly joy out - burst. Al - le - lu - ia!
3. The three sad days are quick - ly sped;
   He ris - es glo - rious from the dead; All glo - ry to our ris - en Head! Al - le - lu - ia!
4. Lord, by the stripes which wound - ed thee,
   From death's dread sting thy serv — ants free, That we may live and sing to thee, Al - le - lu - ia! A - men.

HYMN TUNE: PALESTRINA

35

CROWN HIM WITH MANY CROWNS

The text of this hymn can be attributed to both Matthew Bridges and Godfrey Thring. The hymn tune "Diademata" was written by George J. Elvey in 1868, and it is still by far the most popular choice to accompany this text.

Matthew Bridges
Alt. Godfrey Thring

George J. Elvey

1. Crown him with man-y crowns, The Lamb up-on his throne!
2. Crown him the Lord of life Who tri-umphed o'er the grave,
3. Crown him the Lord of peace Whose power a scep-ter sways
4. Crown him the Lord of love; Be-hold his hands and side,

Hark! How the heaven-ly an-them drowns All mu-sic but its own!
And rose vic-to-rious in the strife For those he came to save!
From pole to pole, that wars may cease And all be prayer and praise!
Those wounds, yet vis-i-ble a-bove, In beau-ty glo-ri-fied:

A-wake, my soul, and sing Of him who died for thee,
His glo-ries now we sing Who died and rose on high:
His reign shall know no end, And round his pierc-ed feet
All hail, Re-deem-er, hail! For thou hast died for me:

And hail him as thy match-less King through all e-ter-ni-ty.
Who died, e-ter-nal life to bring, And lives that death may die.
Fair flowers of par-a-dise ex-tend Their fra-grance ev-er sweet.
Thy praise and glo-ry shall not fail Through-out e-ter-ni-ty. A-men.

HYMN TUNE: DIADEMATA

36

LOVE DIVINE, ALL LOVES EXCELLING

Charles Wesley wrote over 6,500 hymns of which 500 are still used. After his conversion experience, he became a fervent, passionately dedicated Christian, and these qualities can be readily seen in this great hymn which expresses joy and the urgency he felt in telling others about Christ.

Charles Wesley

John Zundel

1. Love di-vine, all loves ex-cel-ling, Joy of heaven, to earth come down:
2. Breathe, O breathe thy lov-ing Spir-it In-to ev-ery trou-bled breast!
3. Come, Al-might-y to de-liv-er, Let us all thy grace re-ceive;
4. Fin-ish, then, thy new cre-a-tion; Pure and spot-less let us be;

Fix in us thy hum-ble dwell-ing, All thy faith-ful mer-cies crown!
Let us all in thee in-her-it; Let us find the prom-ised rest.
Sud-den-ly re-turn, and nev-er, Nev-er more thy tem-ples leave.
Let us see thy great sal-va-tion Per-fect-ly re-stored in thee:

Je-sus, thou art all com-pas-sion, Pure, un-bound-ed love thou art;
Take a-way the love of sin-ning; Al-pha and O-meg-a be;
Thee we would be al-ways bless-ing, Serve thee as thy hosts a-bove,
Change from glo-ry in-to glo-ry, Till in heaven we take our place,

Vis-it us with thy sal-va-tion, En-ter ev-ery trem-bling heart.
End of faith, as its be-gin-ning, Set our hearts at lib-er-ty.
Pray, and praise thee with-out ceas-ing, Glo-ry in thy per-fect love.
Till we cast our crowns be-fore thee, Lost in won-der, love, and praise. A-men.

HYMN TUNE: BEECHER

BREATHE ON ME, BREATH OF GOD

Edwin Hatch

Robert Jackson

1. Breathe on me, Breath of God; Fill me with life a - new, That I may love what thou dost love and do what thou wouldst do.
2. Breathe on me, Breath of God, Un - til my heart is pure, Un - til with thee I will one will, To do and to en - dure.
3. Breathe on me, Breath of God, Till I am whol - ly thine, Un - til this earth - ly part of me Glows with thy fire di - vine.
4. Breathe on me, Breath of God; So shall I nev - er die, But live with thee the per - fect life Of thine e - ter - ni - ty. A - men.

HYMN TUNE: TRENTHAM

SPIRIT OF GOD, DESCEND UPON MY HEART

George Croly

Frederick Atkinson

1. Spir - it of God, de - scend up - on my heart; Wean it from earth; through all its puls - es move; Stoop to my weak - ness, might - y as thou art, And make me love thee as I ought to love.
2. Hast thou not bid us love thee, God and King? All, all thine own - soul, heart, and strength, and mind. I see thy cross - there teach my heart to cling: O let me seek thee, and O let me find!
3. Teach me to feel that thou art al - ways nigh; Teach me the strug - gles of the soul to bear, To check the ris - ing doubt, the reb - el sigh; Teach me the pa - tience of un - an - swered prayer.
4. Teach me to love thee as thine an - gels love, One ho - ly pas - sion fill - ing all my frame; The bap - tism of the heaven - de - scend - ed Dove, My heart an al - tar, and thy love the flame. A - men.

HYMN TUNE. MORECAMBE

38

The Christian Faith

What better way is there to tell of our faith in God than with song? The hymns in this section give us countless opportunities and reasons for praising God. They give the believer assurance of an eternal joy as well as a place of rest for those who remain faithful to the end. Throughout history that faith has made it possible for Daniel to triumph in the lion's den, for Job to keep believing in the midst of trials, for Paul to walk great distances professing Christ's love, and that same faith makes us as today's Christians live as Jesus would have us. Faith is an elusive quality, but as it says in Hebrews 11:1, "Faith is the substance of things hoped for, the evidence of things not seen."

I WILL LOVE THEE

The tune "Hymn to Joy" was taken from the Fourth Movement of Ludwig van Beethoven's "Ninth Symphony" which is often called the "Chorale Symphony". Beethoven was one of the greatest composers who ever lived, and the impact of his work will be felt for centuries to come. This particular text is based on Psalm 18.

Pamela C. Bye
Words based on Psalm 18

Arr. from Ludwig van Beethoven
by Edward Hodges

HYMN TUNE: HYMN TO JOY

GLORIOUS THINGS OF THEE ARE SPOKEN

This majestic tune was composed by Franz Joseph Haydn because the Chancellor of Austria wanted an Austrian hymn which would be admired as much as the highly-praised "God Save the King". Haydn also used this melody in his "Emperor String Quartet". The hymn text by John Newton was based on Isaiah 33: 20 & 21.

John Newton

Franz Joseph Haydn

1. Glo - rious things of thee are spo - ken, Zi - on, cit - y of our God;
2. See, the streams of liv - ing wa - ters, Spring-ing from e - ter - nal Love,
3. Round each hab - i - ta - tion hov-ering, See the cloud and fire ap-pear

He whose word can - not be bro - ken Formed thee for his own a - bode:
Well sup - ply thy sons and daugh-ters, And all fear of want re - move:
For a glo - ry and a cov - ering, Show - ing that the Lord is near!

On the Rock of A - ges found - ed, What can shake thy sure re-pose?
Who can faint while such a riv - er Ev - er will their thirst as-suage?
Glo rious things of thee are spo - ken, Zi - on, cit - y of our God;

With sal - va-tion's walls sur-round-ed, Thou mayest smile at all thy foes.
Grace which, like the Lord, the Giv - er, Nev - er fails from age to age.
He, whose word can - not be bro - ken Formed thee for his own a-bode. A - men.

HYMN TUNE: AUSTRIAN HYMN

41

DAILY, DAILY SING THE PRAISES

Sabine Baring-Gould, famous nineteenth century poet, wrote the text for this hymn. An original chorus was added by William A. Bay who also composed this tune in 1980.

Verses by Sabine Baring-Gould
Chorus by William Bay

William Bay

1. Dai - ly, dai - ly sing the prais - es Of the Cit - y God hath made;
2. In the midst of that dear Cit - y Christ is reign - ing on His seat,
3. From the throne a riv - er is - sues, clear as crys - tal, pas - sing bright,
4. There the wind is sweet - ly frag - rant, And is la - den with the song

In the beau - teous fields of Ed - en Its foun - da - tion stones are laid. Sing
And the an - gels swing their cen - sers In a ring a - bout His feet.
And it tra - ver - ses the Cit - y Like a sud - den beam of light.
Of the ser - aphs, and the el - ders, And the great re - deem - ed throng.

glo - ry un - to our Cit-y of Zi - on, Praise the Cit - y of our King. The

heav'n - ly hosts sing, "Al - le - lu - ia!" Glo - ry and hon - or we bring.

THE CHURCH'S ONE FOUNDATION

The text of this stately hymn was written by Samuel J. Stone, an Anglican clergyman, in the mid nineteenth century. The hymn tune "Aurelia" was composed by Samuel Sebastian Wesley, grandson of the great English evangelist, Charles Wesley. Samuel S. Wesley was the greatest organist of his day, and he wrote extensive vocal and instrumental compositions.

Samuel J. Stone

Samuel Sebastian Wesley

1. The church-'s one foun - da - tion Is Je - sus Christ her Lord;
2. E - lect from ev - ery na - tion, Yet one o'er all the earth,
3. 'Mid toil and trib - u - la - tion And tu - mult of her war,
4. Yet she on earth hath un - ion With Fa - ther, Spir - it, Son,

She is his new cre - a - tion By wa - ter and the word:
Her char - ter of sal - va - tion One Lord, one faith, one birth;
She waits the con - sum - ma - tion Of peace for ev - er - more;
And mys - tic sweet com - mun - ion With those whose rest is won:

From heaven he came and sought her To be his ho - ly bride;
One ho - ly name she bless - es, Par - takes one ho - ly food,
Till, with the vi - sion glo - rious, Her long - ing eyes are blest,
O hap - py ones and ho - ly! Lord, give us grace that we,

With his own blood he bought her, And for her life he died.
And to one hope she press - es With ev - ery grace en - dued.
And the great church vic - to - rious Shall be the church at rest.
Like them, the meek and low - ly, On high may dwell with thee. A - men.

HYMN TUNE: AURELIA

BREAD OF THE WORLD

This hymn is a favorite for use during Communion because it so beautifully describes the Sacrament and expresses the gratitude which the Christian feels for Christ's passion, death, and resurrection without which there would be no hope for mankind.

Reginald Heber

J. S. Bach Hodges

1. Bread of the world in mer - cy bro - ken, Wine of the
2. Look on the heart by sor - row bro - ken, Look on the

soul in mer - cy shed, By whom the words of
tears by sin - ners shed, And be thy feast to

life were spo-ken, And in whose death our sins are dead:
us the to-ken That by thy grace our souls are fed. A - men.

HYMN TUNE: EUCHARISTIC HYMN

......Jesus took bread, and blessed it, and brake it, and gave it to the disciples, and said, Take, eat; this is my body. And he took the cup, and gave thanks, and gave it to them saying, Drink ye all of it; for this is my blood of the new testament, which is shed for many for the remission of sins.

Matthew 26:26-28

O SACRED HEAD NOW WOUNDED

The original text of this great passion chorale of the twelfth century was in Latin, consequently, the hymn has been translated by a number of authors both German and English. The hymn tune "Passion Chorale" was composed by Hans Leo Hassler, an accomplished German composer of the late sixteenth century. The tune was a favorite of Johann Sebastian Bach, the greatest of all Baroque composers, who used it repeatedly in his "St. Matthew Passion".

Old Latin hymn
James W. Alexander, Eng. tr.

Hans Leo Hassler
Arr. by Johann Sebastian Bach

1. O sa-cred Head, now wound-ed, With grief and shame weighed down,
2. What thou, my Lord, hast suf-fered Was all for sin-ners' gain:
3. What lan-guage shall I bor-row To thank thee, dear-est Friend,

Now scorn-ful-ly sur-round-ed With thorns, thine on-ly crown;
Mine, mine was the trans-gres-sion, But thine the dead-ly pain.
For this thy dy-ing sor-row, Thy pit-y with-out end?

How pale thou art with an-guish, With sore a-buse and scorn!
Lo, here I fall, my Sav-ior! 'Tis I de-serve thy place;
O make me thine for-ev-er, And should I faint-ing be,

How does that vis-age lan-guish Which once was bright as morn!
Look on me with thy fa-vor; Vouch-safe to me thy grace.
Lord, let me nev-er, nev-er Out-live my love to thee. A-men.

HYMN TUNE: PASSION CHORALE

45

MY FAITH LOOKS UP TO THEE

Lowell Mason, who lived in the 1800's, had perhaps his greatest influence in the teaching of singing to children. Mason composed many famous hymn tunes, and was a dominant factor in church and school music for at least sixty years. Ray Palmer was a Congregational minister, and he authored many religious poems and essays.

Ray Palmer   Lowell Mason

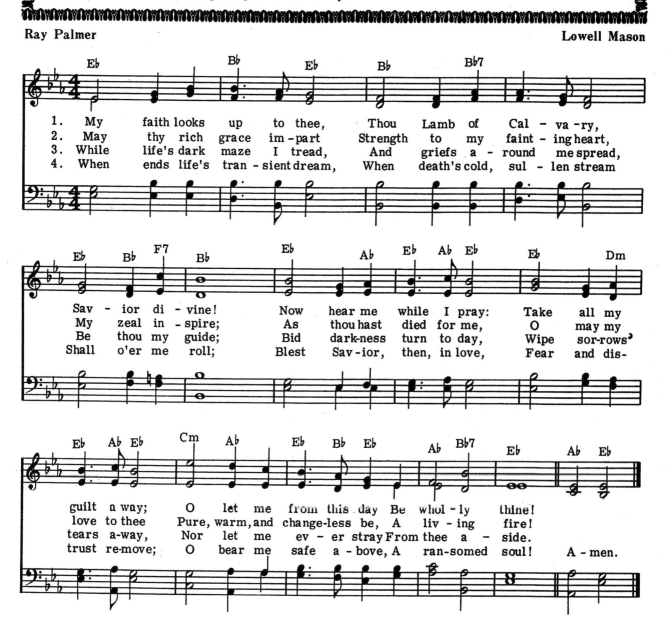

HYMN TUNE: OLIVET

Be strong and of a good courage; be not afraid, neither be thou dismayed: for the Lord thy God is with thee whithersoever thou goest.

Joshua 1:9

ROCK OF AGES

This is one of the greatest evangelical hymns ever written, and it is a favorite of practically every denomination. It speaks of Christ, the rock, as the protector of all true believers, and the hymn gives comfort and assurance to all Christians. Thomas Hastings, composer of the hymn tune, wrote over 600 hymn texts and composed at least 1000 hymn tunes. He felt that whether in speech or song, God deserved the very best of our abilities in His praise. The text of the hymn was written by Augustus M. Toplady, a powerful and dedicated preacher of eighteenth century England.

Augustus M. Toplady

Thomas Hastings

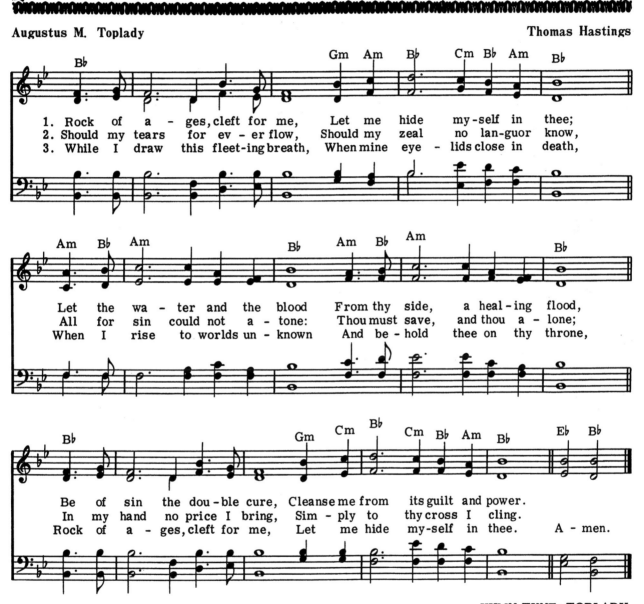

1. Rock of a - ges, cleft for me, Let me hide my-self in thee;
2. Should my tears for ev - er flow, Should my zeal no lan-guor know,
3. While I draw this fleet-ing breath, When mine eye - lids close in death,

Let the wa - ter and the blood From thy side, a heal-ing flood,
All for sin could not a - tone: Thou must save, and thou a - lone;
When I rise to worlds un - known And be - hold thee on thy throne,

Be of sin the dou - ble cure, Cleanse me from its guilt and power.
In my hand no price I bring, Sim - ply to thy cross I cling.
Rock of a - ges, cleft for me, Let me hide my-self in thee. A - men.

HYMN TUNE: TOPLADY

And God is able to make all grace abound toward you; that ye, always having all sufficiency in all things, may abound to every good word......Thanks be to God for his unspeakable gift.

II. Corinthians 9:8&15

Thou hast made us for Thyself, O God, and our hearts are restless until they rest in thee.

St. Augustine

LEANING ON THE EVERLASTING ARMS

This early nineteenth century gospel song is a favorite of many since it expresses the safety and security which are available in the "arms of Jesus".

Elisha Hoffman   Anthony Showalter

1. What a fel-low-ship, what a joy di-vine, Lean-ing on the ev-er-last-ing arms;
2. Oh, how sweet to walk in this pilgrim way, Lean-ing on the ev-er-last-ing arms;
3. What have I to dread, what have I to fear, Lean-ing on the ev-er-last-ing arms?

What a bless-ed-ness, what a peace is mine, Lean-ing on the ev-er-last-ing arms.
Oh, how bright the path grows from day to day, Lean-ing on the ev-er-last-ing arms.
I have bless-ed peace with my Lord so near, Lean-ing on the ev-er-last-ing arms.

Refrain

Lean - ing, lean - ing, Safe and secure from all a-larms;
Lean-ing on Je-sus, lean-ing on Je-sus,

Lean - ing, lean - ing, Lean-ing on the ev-er-last-ing arms.
Lean-ing on Je-sus, lean-ing on Je-sus,

HYMN TUNE: SHOWALTER

COME, THOU FOUNT OF EVERY BLESSING

Robert Robinson

American Folk Tune

1. Come, thou Fount of ev - ery bless - ing, Tune my heart to sing thy grace;
2. Here I raise mine Eb - e - ne - zer; Hith - er by thy help I'm come;
3. O to grace how great a debt - or Dai - ly I'm con - strained to be!

Streams of mer - cy, nev - er ceas - ing, Call for songs of loud - est praise.
And I hope, by thy good pleas - ure, Safe - ly to ar - rive at home.
Let thy good - ness, like a fet - ter, Bind my wan - dering heart to thee:

Teach me some me - lo - dious son - net, Sung by flam - ing tongues a - bove;
Je - sus sought me when a stran - ger, Wan - dering from the fold of God;
Prone to wan - der, Lord, I feel it, Prone to leave the God I love;

Praise the mount! I'm fixed up - on it, Mount of thy re - deem - ing love.
He, to res - cue me from dan - ger, In - ter - posed his pre - cious blood.
Here's my heart, O take and seal it, Seal it for thy courts a - bove. A - men.

HYMN TUNE: NETTLETON

I can do all things through Christ which strengtheneth me.
Philippians 4:13

JESUS, LOVER OF MY SOUL

Charles Wesley's text for this hymn was felt by some people in the 1700's to be too intimate, so it was not used in most hymnals until after 1800. Much comfort can be gained from this text because it expresses the complete faith and trust which the Christian places in Christ. The hymn tune "Martyn" was written in 1834 by Simeon Marsh, a singing teacher in New York State.

Charles Wesley   Simeon B. Marsh

HYMN TUNE: MARTYN

HEAVENLY FATHER, WE APPRECIATE YOU

Source Unknown

HOW SWEET THE NAME OF JESUS SOUNDS

John Newton   Alexander Reinagle

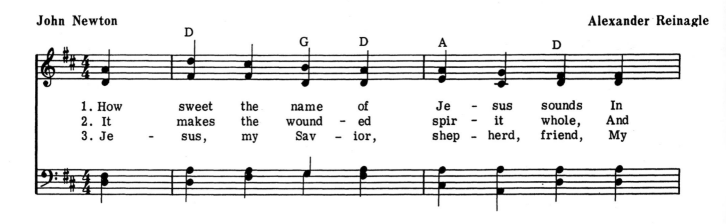

1. How sweet the name of Je - sus sounds In
2. It makes the wound - ed spir - it whole, And
3. Je - sus, my Sav - ior, shep - herd, friend, My

a be - liev - er's ear! It soothes his sor - rows,
calms the trou - bled breast; 'Tis man - na to the
pro - phet, priest, and king, My Lord, my life, my

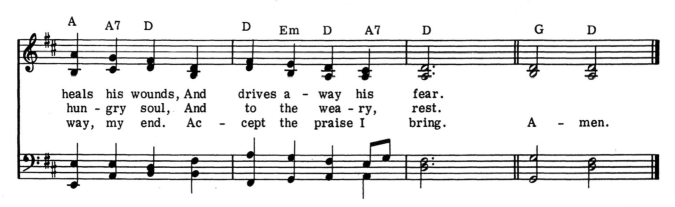

heals his wounds, And drives a - way his fear.
hun - gry soul, And to the wea - ry, rest.
way, my end. Ac - cept the praise I bring. A - men.

HYMN TUNE: ST. PETER

Saviour, where'er thy steps I see; Dauntless, untired, I follow thee: O let thy hand support
me still; And lead me to thy holy hill!

- N. L. Von Zinzendorf, 1721

THERE'S SOMETHING ABOUT THAT NAME

Gloria Gaither and
William J. Gaither

William J. Gaither

THERE IS A NAME I LOVE TO HEAR

Frederick Whitfield

Anonymous

1. There is a name I love to hear, I love to sing its worth;
2. It tells me of a Sav-iour's love, Who died to set me free;
3. It tells me what my Fa-ther hath In store for ev-'ry day,
4. It tells of One whose lov-ing heart Can feel my deep-est woe,

It sounds like mu-sic in mine ear, The sweet-est name on earth.
It tells me of His pre-cious blood, The sin-ner's per-fect plea.
And though I tread a dark-some path, Yields sun-shine all the way.
Who in each sor-row bears a part, That none can bear be-low.

REFRAIN

Oh, how I love Je - sus, Oh, how I love Je - sus,

Oh, how I love Je - sus, Be-cause He first loved me.

HYMN TUNE: OH, HOW I LOVE JESUS

Is any among you afflicted? Let him pray. Is any merry? Let him sing psalms.

James 5:13

ONLY TRUST HIM

John Stockton

John Stockton

1. Come, ev-'ry soul by sin op-pressed, There's mer-cy with the Lord,
2. For Je-sus shed His pre-cious blood Rich blessings to be-stow;
3. Yes, Je-sus is the truth, the way, That leads you in-to rest;
4. Come, then, and join this ho-ly band, And on to glo-ry go,

And He will sure-ly give you rest By trust-ing in His word.
Plunge now in-to the crim-son flood That wash-es white as snow.
Be-lieve in Him with-out de-lay, And you are ful-ly blest.
To dwell in that ce-les-tial land, Where joys im-mor-tal flow.

REFRAIN

On-ly trust Him, on-ly trust Him, on-ly trust Him now;

He will save you, He will save you, He will save you now.

HYMN TUNE: STOCKTON

Have mercy upon me, O God, according to thy lovingkindness: according unto the multitude of thy tender mercies blot out my transgressions. Wash me thoroughly from mine iniquity and cleanse me from my sin.

Psalm 51:1&2

PASS ME NOT, O GENTLE SAVIOUR

Fanny Crosby

William Doane

1. Pass me not, O gen-tle Sav-iour, Hear my hum-ble cry;
2. Let me at Thy throne of mer-cy Find a sweet re-lief;
3. Trust-ing on-ly in Thy mer-it, Would I seek Thy face;
4. Thou the spring of all my com-fort, More than life to me,

While on oth-ers Thou art call-ing, Do not pass me by.
Kneel-ing there in deep con-tri-tion, Help my un-be-lief.
Heal my wound-ed, bro-ken spir-it, Save me by Thy grace.
Whom have I on earth be-side Thee? Whom in heav'n but Thee?

REFRAIN

Sav-iour, Sav-iour, Hear my hum-ble cry;

While on oth-ers Thou art call-ing, Do not pass me by.

HYMN TUNE: PASS ME NOT

That if thou shalt confess with thy mouth the Lord Jesus, and shalt believe in thine heart that God hath raised him from the dead, thou shalt be saved. For with the heart man believeth unto righteousness; and with the mouth confession is made unto salvation.

Romans 10:9&10

AMAZING GRACE

The tune of "Amazing Grace" is an early American melody whose source is unknown. This hymn, which has always been popular in the church, gained new levels of widespread popularity during the 1970's when it was recorded by the well-known folksinger Judy Collins. After an unhappy youth, John Newton, who composed the text, became the owner of his own slave ship at the age of twenty-three. During a violent ocean storm, Newton feared for the lives of himself and his crew, and he cried out to God for protection. The sea was calmed, and Newton took this as a sign that he should turn from his life of sin to spread the Gospel. He then became one of the best of the evangelical clergymen of eighteenth century England.

John Newton Early American melody

HYMN TUNE: AMAZING GRACE

I will sing of mercy and judgment; unto thee, O Lord, will I sing.
Psalm 101:1

Speaking to yourselves in psalms, and hymns, and spiritual songs, singing and making melody in your heart to the Lord.

Ephesians 5:19

BECAUSE HE LIVES

Gloria Gaither and
William J. Gaither

William J. Gaither

1. God sent His Son they call Him Je - sus,
2. How sweet to hold a new - born ba - by,
3. And then one day I'll cross the riv - er,

He came to love, heal and for - give;
And feel the pride and joy he gives;
I'll fight life's fi - nal war with pain;

He lived and died to buy my par - don,
But great - er still the calm as - sur - ance:
And then, as death gives way to vic - t'ry,

An emp - ty grave is there to prove my Sav - ior lives.
This child can face un - cer - tain days be - cause Christ lives.
I'll see the lights of glo - ry and I'll know He lives.

Chorus

Be - cause He lives I can face to - mor - row,

Be - cause He lives all fear is gone;

Be - cause I know I know He has the fu - ture

And life is worth the liv - ing just be - cause He lives.

WHAT A FRIEND WE HAVE IN JESUS

This hymn was written to offer comfort and solace to anyone suffering or in despair. The text by the Irish educator Joseph Scriven was explained by the author as written by "the Lord and myself together". Charles Converse was a famous American lawyer who also was a composer of symphonies, hymns, overtures, and several string quartets.

Joseph Scriven

Charles Converse

1. What a friend we have in Je - sus, All our sins and griefs to bear!
2. Have we tri-als and temp-ta - tions? Is there trou-ble an - y - where?
3. Are we weak and heav-y - la - den, Cum-bered with a load of care?

What a priv-i-lege to car - ry Ev - ery-thing to God in prayer!
We should nev-er be dis-cour - aged; Take it to the Lord in prayer.
Pre - cious Sav-ior, still our ref - uge— Take it to the Lord in prayer.

Oh what peace we of - ten for - feit, Oh what need-less pain we bear.
Can we find a friend so faith - ful Who will all our sor-rows share?
Do thy friends de-spise, for-sake thee? Take it to the Lord in prayer!

All be-cause we do not car - ry Ev - ery-thing to God in prayer.
Je - sus knows our ev - ery weak - ness; Take it to the Lord in prayer!
In his arms he'll take and shield thee; Thou wilt find a sol-ace there. A - men.

HYMN TUNE: ERIE

CHRIST BE BESIDE ME

St. Patrick

Gaelic Melody

1. Christ be be-side me, Christ be be-fore me, Christ be be-hind me, King of my heart.
2. Christ on my right hand, Christ on my left hand, Christ all a-round me, shield in the strife.
3. Christ be in all hearts think-ing a-bout me, Christ be on all tongues tell-ing of me.

Christ be with-in me, Christ in my sleep-ing, Christ be the vis-ion

Christ be be-low me, Christ be a-bove me, nev-er to part.
Christ in my sit-ting, Christ in my ris-ing, light of my life.
in eyes that see me; in ears that hear me, Christ ev-er be.

JESUS IS THE SWEETEST NAME I KNOW

Je-sus is the sweetest name I know, And He's just the same as His love-ly name, And that's the rea-son why I love Him so; Oh, Je-sus is the sweet-est name I know.

SAVIOR, AGAIN TO THY DEAR NAME WE RAISE

John Ellerton

Edward J. Hopkins

1. Sav - ior, a - gain to thy dear name we raise
2. Grant us thy peace up - on our home-ward way;
3. Grant us thy peace, Lord, through the com - ing night;
4. Grant us thy peace through - out our earth - ly life;

With one ac - cord our part - ing hymn of praise;
With thee be - gan, with thee shall end the day:
Turn thou for us its dark - ness in - to light;
Peace to thy church from er - ror and from strife;

Once more we bless thee ere our wor - ship cease,
Guard thou the lips from sin, the hearts from shame,
From harm and dan - ger keep thy chil - dren free,
Peace to our land, the fruit of truth and love;

As in our hearts we wait thy word of peace.
That in this house have called up - on thy name.
For dark and light are both a - like to thee.
Peace in each heart, thy Spir - it from a - bove. A - men.

HYMN TUNE: ELLERS

. . . . . . And they sang praises with gladness, and they bowed their heads and worshipped.
II. Chronicles 29:30

And when they had sung an hymn, they went out into the mount of Olives.
Matthew 26:30

The Christian Life

These hymns show us that salvation is only the beginning for a truly dedicated Christian. Following the initial surrendering of one's life to Christ comes the diligent and unceasing striving toward Christian perfection which the Bible demands. Matthew 5:48 tells us, "Be ye therefore perfect, even as your Father which is in Heaven is perfect". It is difficult to live a Christian life, for to do so often involves standing alone and being different from those around us. This task is impossible unless one depends on Christ for the strength which he has promised.

HOW FIRM A FOUNDATION

The early American melody shown here with this text is just one of the many hymn tunes which has been used through the years. The text explains what is expected of a Christian-- never waivering trust in God and His continual presence.

"K" in Rippon's A Selection of Hymns

Early American melody

1. How firm a foun - da - tion, ye saints of the Lord,
2. "Fear not, I am with thee! O be not dis - mayed,
3. "When through the deep wat - ers I call thee to go,
4. "The soul that on Je - sus hath leaned for re - pose,

Is laid for your faith in his ex - cel - lent word!
For I am thy God, and will still give thee aid;
The riv - ers of sor - row shall not o - ver - flow;
I will not, I will not de - sert to his foes;

What more can he say than to you he hath said,
I'll strength - en thee, help thee, and cause thee to stand,
For I will be with thee, thy trou - bles to bless,
That soul, though all hell should en - deav - or to shake,

To you who for ref - uge to Je - sus have fled?
Up - held by my right - eous, om - nip - o - tent hand.
And sanc - ti - fy to thee thy deep - est dis - tress.
I'll nev - er, no nev - er, no nev - er for - sake!"   A - men.

HYMN TUNE: FOUNDATION

O LOVE THAT WILT NOT LET ME GO

George Matheson

Albert Peace

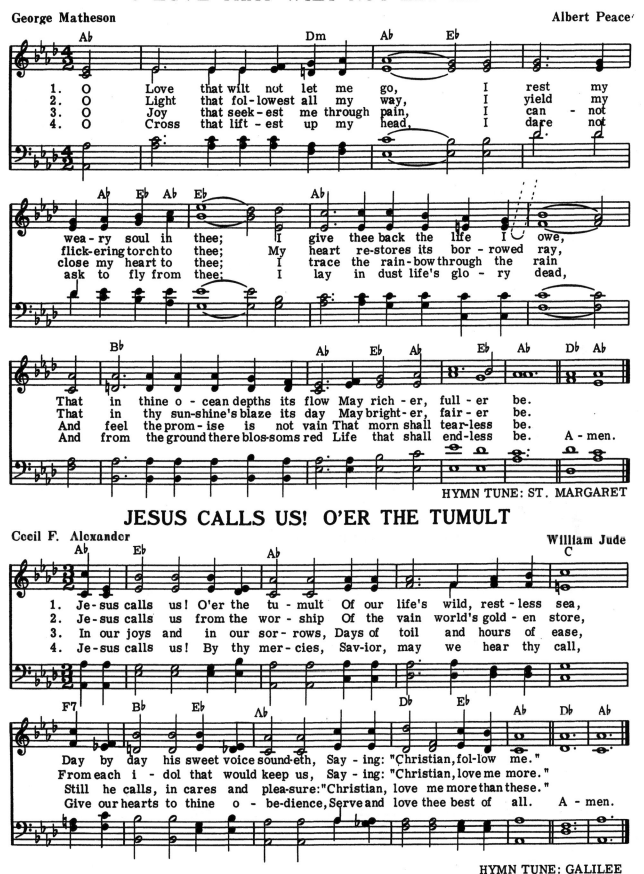

1. O Love that wilt not let me go, I rest my
2. O Light that fol-lowest all my way, I yield my
3. O Joy that seek-est me through pain, I can-not
4. O Cross that lift-est up my head, I dare not

wea-ry soul in thee; I give thee back the life I owe,
flick-ering torch to thee; My heart re-stores its bor-rowed ray,
close my heart to thee; I trace the rain-bow through the rain
ask to fly from thee; I lay in dust life's glo-ry dead,

That in thine o-cean depths its flow May rich-er, full-er be.
That in thy sun-shine's blaze its day May bright-er, fair-er be.
And feel the prom-ise is not vain That morn shall tear-less be.
And from the ground there blos-soms red Life that shall end-less be. A-men.

HYMN TUNE: ST. MARGARET

JESUS CALLS US! O'ER THE TUMULT

Cecil F. Alexander

William Jude

1. Je-sus calls us! O'er the tu-mult Of our life's wild, rest-less sea,
2. Je-sus calls us from the wor-ship Of the vain world's gold-en store,
3. In our joys and in our sor-rows, Days of toil and hours of ease,
4. Je-sus calls us! By thy mer-cies, Sav-ior, may we hear thy call,

Day by day his sweet voice sound-eth, Say-ing: "Christian, fol-low me."
From each i-dol that would keep us, Say-ing: "Christian, love me more."
Still he calls, in cares and plea-sure: "Christian, love me more than these."
Give our hearts to thine o-be-dience, Serve and love thee best of all. A-men.

HYMN TUNE: GALILEE

65

ONWARD CHRISTIAN SOLDIERS

Sabine Baring–Gould

Arthur Sullivan

1. On-ward, Christian sol - diers, March-ing as to war, With the cross of Je - sus Go - ing on be - fore! Christ, the roy - al Mas - ter, Leads a - gainst the foe; For-ward in - to bat - tle, See, his ban-ners go.

2. At the sign of tri - umph Sa - tan's host doth flee; On, then, Christian sol - diers, On to vic-to - ry! Hell's foun-da-tions quiv - er At the shout of praise; Broth-ers, lift your voic - es, Loud your an-thems raise.

3. Like a migh-ty ar - my Moves the Church of God; Broth-ers, we are tread - ing Where the saints have trod; We are not di - vid - ed, All one bo - dy we, One in hope and doc - trine, One in cha - ri - ty.

4. On-ward, then, ye peo - ple, Join our hap - py throng; Blend with ours your voi - ces In the tri - umph song. Glo - ry, laud, and ho - nor, Un - to Christ the King; This through countless a - ges men and an-gels sing.

Refrain

On - ward, Chris-tian sol - diers, March-ing as to war, With the cross of Je - sus Go - ing on be - fore! A - men.

HYMN TUNE: ST. GERTRUDE

66

STAND UP; STAND UP FOR JESUS

George Duffield, the noted Presbyterian minister, wrote the text of this hymn after being with a dying friend whose last words were, "Tell them to stand up for Jesus." Duffield also used Ephesians 6:14 as a reference, "Stand therefore, having your loins girt about with truth, and having on the breastplate of righteousness."

George Duffield

George J. Webb

1. Stand up, stand up for Je - sus, Ye sol - diers of the cross;
2. Stand up, stand up for Je - sus; The trum - pet call o - bey;
3. Stand up, stand up for Je - sus; The strife will not be long;

Lift high his roy - al ban - ner; It must not suf - fer loss:
Forth to the might - y con - flict In this his glo - rious day:
This day the noise of bat - tle, The next the vic - tor's song:

From vic - tory un - to vic - tory His ar - my shall he lead.
Put on the gos - pel ar - mor; Each piece put on with prayer.
To him that o - ver - com - eth, A crown of life shall be;

Till ev - ery foe is van - quished, And Christ is Lord in - deed.
Where du - ty calls, or dan - ger, Be nev - er want-ing there.
He with the King of glo - ry Shall reign e - ter - nal - ly. A - men.

HYMN TUNE: WEBB

67

LORD, I WANT TO BE A CHRISTIAN

Spiritual

HYMN TUNE: I WANT TO BE A CHRISTIAN

Yet if any man suffer as a Christian, let him not be ashamed; but let him glorify God on this behalf. For the time is come that judgment must begin at the house of God: and if it first begin at us, what shall the end be of them that obey not the gospel of God? And if the righteous scarcely be saved, where shall the ungodly and the sinner appear? Wherefore let them that suffer according to the will of God commit the keeping of their souls to him in well doing, as unto a faithful Creator.

I. Peter 4:16-19

TAKE MY LIFE, AND LET IT BE

Frances Havergal

Henry Malan

1. Take my life, and let it be Con-se-crat-ed, Lord, to thee. Take my mo-ments and my days; Let them flow in cease-less praise. Let them flow in cease-less praise.
2. Take my hands, and let them move At the im-pulse of thy love. Take my feet and let them be Swift and beau-ti-ful for thee. Swift and beau-ti-ful for thee.
3. Take my lips, and let them be Filled with mes-sa-ges from thee. Take my in-tel-lect, and use Ev-ery power as thou shalt choose. Ev-ery power as thou shalt choose.
4. Take my will, and make it thine; It shall be no long-er mine. Take my heart; it is thine own; It shall be thy roy-al throne. It shall be thy roy-al throne.
5. Take my love; my Lord, I pour At thy feet its trea-sure store. Take my-self, and I will be ev-er, on-ly, all for thee. Ev-er, on-ly, all for thee.

A - men.

HYMN TUNE: HENDON

JUST AS I AM, WITHOUT ONE PLEA

Charlotte Elliott

William Bradbury

1. Just as I am, with-out one plea But that thy blood was shed for me, And that thou biddest me come to thee, O Lamb of God, I come, I come!
2. Just as I am, though tossed a-bout With man-y a con-flict, man-y a doubt; With fears with-in and foes with-out, O Lamb of God, I come, I come!
3. Just as I am, poor, wretch-ed, blind; Sight, rich-es, heal-ing of the mind, Yea, all I need in thee to find, O Lamb of God, I come, I come!
4. Just as I am, thou wilt re-ceive, Wilt wel-come, par-don, cleanse, re-lieve, Be-cause thy prom-ise I be-lieve, O Lamb of God, I come, I come!

A-men.

HYMN TUNE: WOODWORTH

JESUS, KEEP ME NEAR THE CROSS

Fanny Crosby

William Doane

1. Je - sus, keep me near the cross: There a pre - cious foun - tain,
2. Near the cross, a trem - bling soul, Love and mer - cy found me;
3. Near the cross! O Lamb of God, Bring its scenes be - fore me;

Free to all, a heal - ing stream, Flows from Cal - vary's moun - tain.
There the Bright and Morn - ing Star Sheds its beams a - round me.
Help me walk from day to day, With its shad - ow o'er me.

REFRAIN

In the cross, in the cross, Be my glo - ry ev - er,

Till my rap-tured soul shall find Rest be-yond the riv - er. A - men.

HYMN TUNE: NEAR THE CROSS

And, having made peace through the blood of his cross, by him to reconcile all things unto himself; by him, I say, whether they be things in earth, or things in heaven. And you, that were sometime alienated and enemies in your mind by wicked works, yet now hath he reconciled. In the body of his flesh through death, to present you holy and unblamable and unreprovable in his sight:

Colossians 1:20-22

O MASTER, LET ME WALK WITH THEE

The author of this text, Washington Gladden, is unique in that he advocated what we call a "social gospel" before it was fashionable. The second verse speaks of helping those who are headed in the wrong way to find their way to Christ.

Washington Gladden   Henry P. Smith

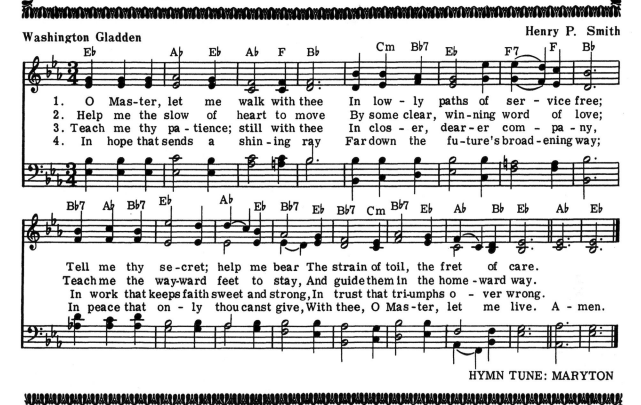

1. O Mas-ter, let me walk with thee In low - ly paths of ser - vice free;
2. Help me the slow of heart to move By some clear, win-ning word of love;
3. Teach me thy pa - tience; still with thee In clos - er, dear-er com - pa - ny,
4. In hope that sends a shin-ing ray Far down the fu-ture's broad-ening way;

Tell me thy se-cret; help me bear The strain of toil, the fret of care.
Teach me the way-ward feet to stay, And guide them in the home-ward way.
In work that keeps faith sweet and strong, In trust that tri-umphs o - ver wrong.
In peace that on - ly thou canst give, With thee, O Mas-ter, let me live. A - men.

HYMN TUNE: MARYTON

LORD, SPEAK TO ME, THAT I MAY SPEAK

The beauty of this text lies in its simplicity and directness. Frances Havergal was a well-respected English poet and philanthropist who accomplished much even though she was plagued by frail health for many years.

Frances Havergal   Robert Schumann

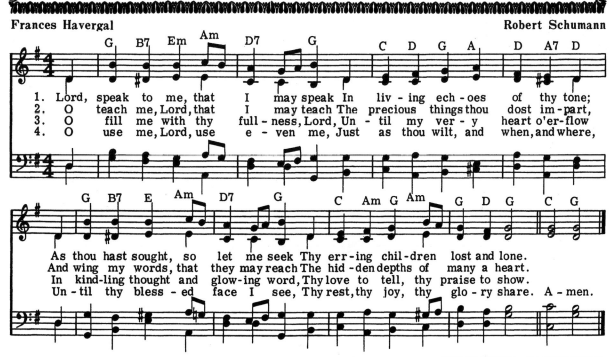

1. Lord, speak to me, that I may speak In liv - ing ech - oes of thy tone;
2. O teach me, Lord, that I may teach The precious things thou dost im - part,
3. O fill me with thy full - ness, Lord, Un - til my ver - y heart o'er-flow
4. O use me, Lord, use e - ven me, Just as thou wilt, and when, and where,

As thou hast sought, so let me seek Thy err-ing chil-dren lost and lone.
And wing my words, that they may reach The hid-den depths of many a heart.
In kind-ling thought and glow-ing word, Thy love to tell, thy praise to show.
Un - til thy bless - ed face I see, Thy rest, thy joy, thy glo - ry share. A - men.

71   HYMN TUNE: CANONBURY

I WOULD BE TRUE

This hymn deals with the importance of Christian living, not only from a personal viewpoint, but also because of the influence we all have on others. The text stresses the responsibility we have for those who might use us as an example.

Howard Walter   Joseph Peek

HYMN TUNE: PEEK

WHEN WE WALK WITH THE LORD

This hymn grew out of one of the early revival meetings of Daniel Moody. A young man came forward during the invitation hymn, and his words were, "I will trust and obey". D.B. Towner, who was musical director at Moody Bible Institute, heard the words, and they became the inspiration for this popular salvation hymn.

John H. Sammis   Daniel B. Towner

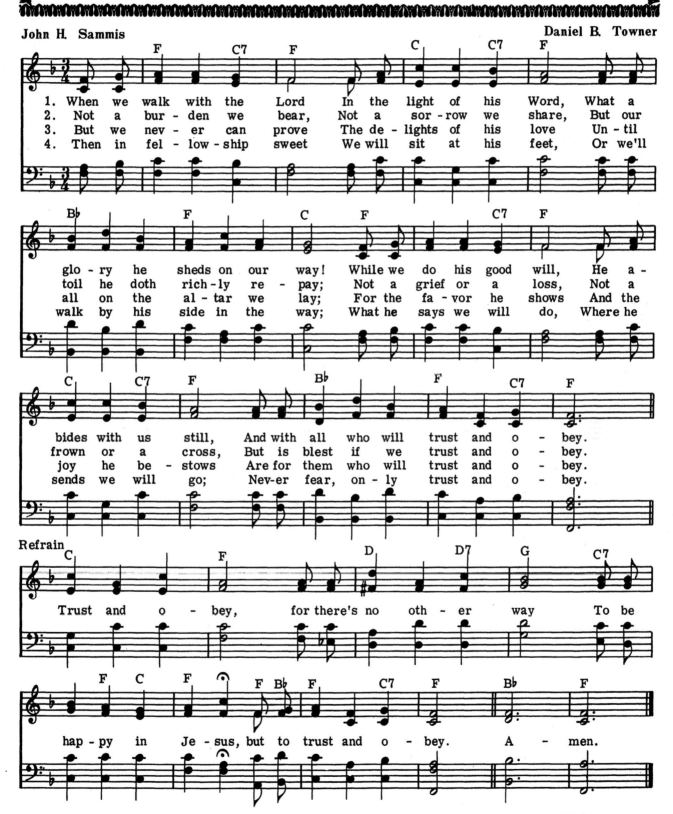

1. When we walk with the Lord In the light of his Word, What a
2. Not a bur-den we bear, Not a sor-row we share, But our
3. But we nev-er can prove The de-lights of his love Un-til
4. Then in fel-low-ship sweet We will sit at his feet, Or we'll

glo-ry he sheds on our way! While we do his good will, He a-
toil he doth rich-ly re-pay; Not a grief or a loss, Not a
all on the al-tar we lay; For the fa-vor he shows And the
walk by his side in the way; What he says we will do, Where he

bides with us still, And with all who will trust and o-bey.
frown or a cross, But is blest if we trust and o-bey.
joy he be-stows Are for them who will trust and o-bey.
sends we will go; Nev-er fear, on-ly trust and o-bey.

Refrain

Trust and o-bey, for there's no oth-er way To be

hap-py in Je-sus, but to trust and o-bey. A-men.

HYMN TUNE: TRUST AND OBEY

I NEED THEE EVERY HOUR

This is a popular hymn for use in revivals because of its repetition of the idea that all Christians, no matter how dedicated, need Christ every hour. It is not possible for the truly committed believer to take a vacation from dependence on God. Annie Hawks was a mother and housewife, doing her usual chores, when the idea for this text came to her. The tune was composed by Robert Lowry, her pastor at Hanson Place Baptist Church.

Annie Hawks   Robert Lowry

1. I need thee ev-ery hour, Most gra - cious Lord;
2. I need thee ev-ery hour; Stay thou near by;
3. I need thee ev-ery hour, In joy or pain;
4. I need thee ev-ery hour; Teach me thy will;
5. I need thee ev-ery hour, Most Ho - ly One;

No ten - der voice like thine Can peace af - ford.
Temp - ta - tions lose their power When thou art nigh.
Come quick - ly and a - bide, Or life is vain.
And thy rich prom-is - es In me ful - fill.
O make me thine in - deed, Thou bless - ed Son.

Refrain

I need thee, O I need thee, Ev - ery hour I need thee;

O bless me now, my Sav - ior, I come to thee! A - men.

HYMN TUNE: NEED

HE LEADETH ME: O BLESSED THOUGHT

Joseph Gilmore, a noted Baptist minister and hymn writer, wrote this text after hearing a sermon on Psalm 23. He was a well-respected writer of poems, editorials, and textbooks, and was for many years professor of English at the University of Rochester. The tune was written by William Bradbury, a famous American musician of the nineteenth century.

Joseph Gilmore   William Bradbury

HYMN TUNE: HE LEADETH ME

TELL ME THE OLD, OLD STORY

Katherine Hankey

William Doane

1. Tell me the old, old sto - ry Of un seen things a - bove,
2. Tell me the sto - ry slow - ly, That I may take it in,
3. Tell me the sto - ry soft - ly, With ear - nest tones, and grave,
4. Tell me the same old sto - ry, When you have cause to fear

Of Je - sus and His glo - ry, Of Je - sus and His love:
That won - der - ful re - demp - tion, God's rem - e - dy for sin!
Re - mem - ber! I'm the sin - ner Whom Je - sus came to save:
That this world's emp - ty glo - ry Is cost - ing me too dear:

Tell me the sto - ry sim - ply, As to a lit - tle child,
Tell me the sto - ry of - ten, For I for - get so soon,
Tell me that sto - ry al - ways, If you would real - ly be,
Yes, and when that world's glo - ry Is dawn - ing on my soul,

For I am weak and wea - ry, And help - less and de - filed.
The ear - ly dew of morn - ing Has passed a - way at noon!
In an - y - time of trou - ble, A com - fort - er to me.
Tell me the old, old sto - ry: "Christ Je - sus makes thee whole."

Tell me the old, old sto - ry, Tell me the old, old sto - ry,

Tell me the old, old sto - ry Of Je - sus and His love.

HYMN TUNE: OLD, OLD STORY

I HAVE DECIDED TO FOLLOW JESUS

Folk melody from India

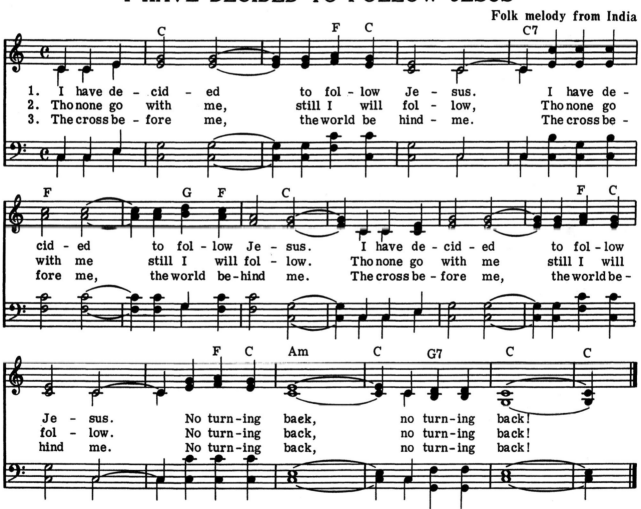

1. I have de - cid - ed to fol - low Je - sus. I have de -
2. Tho none go with me, still I will fol - low, Tho none go
3. The cross be - fore me, the world be hind - me. The cross be -

cid - ed to fol - low Je - sus. I have de - cid - ed to fol - low
with me still I will fol - low. Tho none go with me still I will
fore me, the world be - hind me. The cross be - fore me, the world be -

Je - sus. No turn-ing baek, no turn-ing back!
fol - low. No turn-ing back, no turn-ing back!
hind me. No turn-ing back, no turn-ing back!

My sheep hear my voice, and I know them, and they follow me: And I give unto them eternal life; and they shall never perish, neither shall any man pluck them out of my hand.

John 10:27&28

BLESSED ASSURANCE, JESUS IS MINE

Fanny Crosby, author of over 2000 hymns, composed this great revival song of the nineteenth century. These words stir great emotion and enthusiasm in the heart of a believer as they affirm the message of an eternal glory in Heaven for those who are faithful.

Fanny Crosby

Phoebe Palmer

1. Bless-ed as-sur-ance, Je-sus is mine! O what a fore-taste of glo-ry di-
2. Per-fect sub-mis-sion, per-fect de-light; Vi-sions of rap-ture now burst on my
3. Per-fect sub-mis-sion, all is at rest; I in my Sav-ior am hap-py and

vine! Heir of sal-va-tion, pur-chase of God, Born of his
sight; An-gels de-scend-ing, bring from a-bove Ech-oes of
blest, Watch-ing and wait-ing, look-ing a-bove, Filled with his

Spir-it, washed in his blood. This is my sto-ry, this is my
mer-cy, whis-pers of love.
good-ness, lost in his love.

song, Prais-ing my Sav-ior all the day long; This is my

sto-ry, this is my song, Prais-ing my Sav-ior all the day long. A-men.

HYMN TUNE: ASSURANCE

HE IS LORD

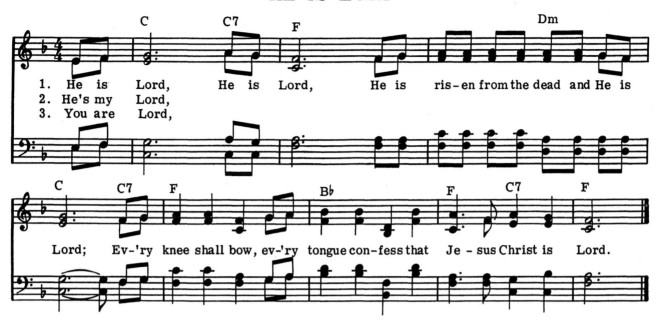

1. He is Lord, He is Lord, He is ris-en from the dead and He is
2. He's my Lord,
3. You are Lord,

Lord; Ev-'ry knee shall bow, ev-'ry tongue con-fess that Je - sus Christ is Lord.

I'VE GOT PEACE LIKE A RIVER

1. I've got peace like a riv - er, I've got peace like a riv - er, I've got
2. I've got joy like a foun-tain, I've got joy like a foun-tain, I've got
3. I've got love like an o - cean, I've got love like an o - cean, I've got

peace like a riv - er in my soul; I've got peace like a riv - er, I've got
joy like a foun-tain in my soul; I've got joy like a foun-tain, I've got
love like an o - cean in my soul; I've got love like an o - cean, I've got

peace like a riv - er, I've got peace like a riv - er in my soul.
joy like a foun-tain, I've got joy like a foun-tain in my soul.
love like an o - cean, I've got love like an o - cean in my soul.

O PERFECT LOVE

This is one of the most popular hymns for use at weddings because of its beautiful words that wish for a newly married couple the perfect life and peace which can be found in a union at whose center is Christ.

Dorothy B. Gurney   Joseph Barnby

1. O per-fect Love, all hu-man thought tran - scend - ing,
2. O per-fect Life, be Thou their full as - sur - ance
3. Grant them the joy which bright-ens earth - ly sor - row;

Low - ly we kneel in prayer be-fore Thy throne,
Of ten-der char - i - ty and stead - fast faith,
Grant them the peace which calms all earth - ly strife,

That theirs may be the love which knows no end - ing,
Of pa - tient hope and qui - et, brave en - dur - ance,
And to life's day the glo-rious un-known mor - row

Whom Thou for - ev - er-more dost join in one.
With child-like trust that fears no pain nor death.
That dawns up - on e - ter - nal love and life. A - men.

HYMN TUNE: O PERFECT LOVE

80

HAPPY THE HOME WHEN GOD IS THERE

Henry Ware, the Younger

John Dykes

1. Hap-py the home when God is there, And love fills ev-ery breast;
2. Hap-py the home when Je-sus' name, Is sweet to ev-ery ear;
3. Hap-py the home when prayer is heard, And praise is wont to rise;
4. Lord, let us in our homes a-gree, This bless-ed peace to gain;

When one their wish and one their prayer, And one their heaven-ly rest.
Where chil-dren ear-ly lisp His fame, And par-ents hold Him dear.
Where par-ents love the sa-cred Word, And all its wis-dom prize.
U-nite our hearts in love to Thee, And love to all will reign, A-men.

HYMN TUNE: ST. AGNES

THE DAY THOU GAVEST, LORD, IS ENDED

John Ellerton

Clement Scholefield

1. The day thou gav-est, Lord, is end-ed; The dark-ness falls at
2. We thank thee that thy church un-sleep-ing, While earth rolls on-ward
3. As o'er each con-ti-nent and is-land, The dawn leads on an-
4. So be it, Lord; thy throne shall nev-er, Like earth's proud em-pires,

thy be-hest; To thee our morn-ing hymns as-cend-ed;
in-to light, Through all the world her watch is keep-ing
oth-er day, The voice of prayer is nev-er si-lent,
pass a-way; Thy king-dom stands and grows for-ev-er

Thy praise shall sanc-ti-fy our rest.
And rests not now by day or night.
Nor die the strains of praise a-way.
Till all thy crea-tures own thy sway. A-men.

HYMN TUNE: ST. CLEMENT

81

ABIDE WITH ME

This hymn, perhaps more than any other, gives comfort to the dying Christian as it presents the brightness Heaven has to offer when earthly life is done. Henry Lyte, the author, suffered from frail health himself, and there are various accounts of the exact time and circumstance under which he wrote this text. Legend has it that this is the hymn sung by those on board the Titanic as it made its descent into the icy waters of the North Atlantic.

Henry Lyte

William Monk

1. A - bide with me: fast falls the e - ven - tide; The dark-ness deep - ens;
2. Swift to its close ebbs out life's lit - tle day; Earth's joys grow dim, its
3. I need Thy pres - ence ev - 'ry pass - ing hour; What but Thy grace can
4. Hold Thou Thy cross be - fore my clos - ing eyes; Shine thro' the gloom, and

Lord, with me a - bide: When oth - er help - ers fail, and com-forts
glo - ries pass a - way; Change and de - cay in all a-round I
foil the tempt-er's pow'r? Who like Thy - self my guide and stay can
point me to the skies: Heav'n's morning breaks and earth's vain shad-ows

flee, Help of the help-less, O a - bide with me!
see: O Thou who chang-est not, a - bide with me!
be? Thro' cloud and sun-shine, O a - bide with me!
flee: In life, in death, O Lord, a - bide with me! A - men.

HYMN TUNE: EVENTIDE

Always bearing about in the body the dying of the Lord Jesus, that the life also of Jesus might be made manifest in our body. For we which live are alway delivered unto death for Jesus' sake, that the life also of Jesus might be made manifest in our mortal flesh. So then death worketh in us, but life in you.

II. Corinthians 4:10-12

The Christian Witness

Christian witness involves our telling others about Christ and the truth which he embodies. The great commission applied not only to the disciples but to all Christians in their everyday lives. Matthew 28: 19 & 20 says, "Go ye therefore, and teach all nations, baptizing them in the name of the Father, and of the Son, and of the Holy Ghost. Teaching them to observe all things whatsoever I have commanded you: and, lo, I am with you always, even unto the end of the world." Many thousands have been influenced by the hymns which are included here. Their texts have always been powerful, and their truth has not changed.

WE PRAISE THEE, O GOD

William Mackay

John Husband

1. We praise Thee, O God! for the Son of Thy love,
2. We praise Thee, O God! for Thy Spir - it of light,
3. All glo - ry and praise to the Lamb that was slain,
4. Re - vive us a - gain· fill each heart with Thy love;

For Je - sus who died, and is now gone a - bove.
Who hath shown us our Sav - iour, and scat - ter'd our night.
Who hath borne all our sins, and hath cleans'd ev - 'ry stain.
May each soul be re - kin - dled with fire from a - bove.

REFRAIN

Hal - le - lu - jah! Thine the glo - ry, Hal - le - lu - jah! a - men;

Hal - le - lu - jah! Thine the glo - ry, Re - vive us a - gain.

HYMN TUNE: REVIVE US AGAIN

The same had not consented to the counsel and deed of them; he was of Arimathaea, a city of the Jews: who also himself waited for the kingdom of God. This man went unto Pilate, and begged the body of Jesus. And he took it down, and wrapped it in linen, and laid it in a sepulchre that was hewn in stone, wherein never man before was laid.

Luke 24:51-53

84

PEACE I GIVE YOU

Bill Bay

Bill Bay

1. "Peace, peace I give you, Not like that you have known._____ Peace, peace I leave you," Je-sus re-ceives you as His own._____
2. Come un-to Je-sus, All whose souls search for rest._____ His yoke is eas-y, Seek Him and sure-ly you'll be blessed._____
3. Je-sus is liv-ing, In our hearts He a-bides._____ God's grace in Je-sus, Sav-ing and fill-ing emp-ty lives._____
4. We sing our praise to God our and Je-sus His Son._____ And with God's Spir-it, Our vic-to-ry has been won._____

BLEST BE THE TIE THAT BINDS

John Fawcett

Johann Naegeli

1. Blest be the tie that binds Our hearts in Chris-tian love: The fel-low-ship of kin-dred minds Is like to that a-bove.
2. Be-fore our Fa-ther's throne We pour our ar-dent prayers; Our fears, our hopes, our aims are one, Our com-forts and our cares.
3. We share each oth-er's woes, Each oth-er's bur-dens bear, And of-ten for each oth-er flows The sym-pa-thiz-ing tear.
4. When we are called to part, it gives us in-ward pain; But we shall still be joined in heart And hope to meet a-gain. A-men.

HYMN TUNE : DENNIS

TELL ME THE STORIES OF JESUS

This song emphasizes the importance of children in the Kingdom of God. The New Testament mentions children learning at Jesus' knee as well as those who led Him into Jerusalem on Palm Sunday. In addition, Christ often taught that a new Christian is like a child and should be nurtured so that he might grow in his faith.

W. H. Parker

F. A. Challinor

1. Tell me the sto-ries of Je - sus I love to hear; Things I would ask Him to tell me If He were here; Scenes by the way - side, Tales of the sea, — Sto - ries of Je - sus, Tell them to me.__

2. First let me hear how the chil - dren Stood 'round His knee; And I shall fan - cy His bless - ing Rest - ing on me;__ Words full of kind - ness, Deeds full of grace All in the love - light Of Je - sus' face.

3. In - to the cit - y I'd fol - low The chil-dren's band, Wav-ing a branch of the palm tree High in my hand; One of His her - alds, Yes I would sing Loud - est ho - san - nas! Je - sus is King.

HYMN TUNE: STORIES OF JESUS

Then were there brought unto him little children, that he should put his hands on them, and pray: and the disciples rebuked them. But Jesus said, Suffer little children, and forbid them not, to come unto me: for of such is the kingdom of heaven. And he laid his hands on them, and departed thence.

Matthew 19:13-15

I LOVE TO TELL THE STORY

Arabella Hankey became interested in the plight of the natives while on a visit to South Africa, and consequently contributed all that she made from her writings to the cause of missions. The text repeats the idea that people never tire of hearing the gospel message preached.

Arabella Hankey

William Fischer

1. I love to tell the story Of unseen things above, Of Jesus and his glory, Of Jesus and his love, I love to tell the story, Because I know 'tis true; It satisfies my longings As nothing else can do.

2. I love to tell the story; 'Tis pleasant to repeat What seems, each time I tell it, More wonderfully sweet. I love to tell the story, For some have never heard The message of salvation From God's own holy Word.

3. I love to tell the story, For those who know it best Seem hungering and thirsting To hear it like the rest. And when, in scenes of glory, I sing the new, new song, 'Twill be the old, old story That I have loved so long.

REFRAIN
I love to tell the story: 'Twill be my theme in glory, To tell the old, old story Of Jesus and his love. A-men.

HYMN TUNE: HANKEY

WHERE CROSS THE CROWDED WAYS OF LIFE

Frank North

William Gardiner

1. Where cross the crowd-ed ways of life, Where sound the
2. In haunts of wretch-ed-ness and need, On shad-owed
3. The cup of wa-ter given for thee Still holds the
4. O Mas-ter, from the moun-tain-side, Make haste to
5. Till sons of men shall learn thy love And fol-low

cries of race and clan A-bove the noise of
thresh-olds dark with fears, From paths where hide the
fresh-ness of thy grace; Yet long these mul-ti-
heal these hearts of pain; A-mong these rest-less
where thy feet have trod; Till, glo-rious from thy

self-ish strife, We hear thy voice, O Son of man!
lures of greed, We catch the vi-sion of thy tears.
tudes to see The sweet com-pas-sion of thy face.
throngs a-bide, O tread the cit-y's streets a-gain,
heaven a-bove, Shall come the cit-y of our God! A-men.

HYMN TUNE: GERMANY

I LOVE THY KINGDOM, LORD

Dwight; Hoadley

Aaron Williams

1. I love thy king-dom, Lord, The house of thine a-bode,
2. For her my tears shall fall, For her my prayers as-cend;
3. Her mis-sion in the world May she ful-fill with zeal:

The church our blessed Re-deem-er saved With his own pre-cious blood.
To her my cares and toils be given Till toils and cares shall end.
Through lov-ing serv-ice where men are, The grace of God re-veal. A-men.

HYMN TUNE: ST.THOMAS

90

LEAD ON, O KING ETERNAL

The hymn tune "Lancashire" was composed in 1836 by Henry Smart, a noted organist and organ designer in England. Ernest W. Shurtleff, who wrote this text, was a minister in various Congregational churches throughout the United States in the early 1900's.

Ernest W. Shurtleff   Henry T. Smart

1. Lead on, O King E - ter - nal! The day of march has come:
2. Lead on, O King E - ter - nal Till sin's fierce war shall cease,
3. Lead on, O King E - ter - nal! We fol - low, not with fears,

Hence - forth in fields of con - quest Thy tents shall be our home.
And ho - li - ness shall whis - per The sweet a - men of peace;
For glad - ness breaks like morn - ing Wher - e'er thy face ap - pears.

Through days of prep - a - ra - tion Thy grace has made us strong,
For not with swords' loud clash - ing Nor roll of stir - ring drums,
Thy cross is lift - ed o'er us; We jour - ney in its light:

And now, O King E - ter - nal, We lift our bat - tle song.
But deeds of love and mer - cy, The heaven - ly king-dom comes.
The crown a - waits the con - quest; Lead on, O God of might. A - men.

HYMN TUNE: LANCASHIRE

91

SOLDIERS OF CHRIST, ARISE

Charles Wesley

George Elvey

HYMN TUNE: DIADEMATA

Finally, my brethren, be strong in the Lord, and in the power of his might. Put on the whole armour of God, that ye may be able to stand against the wiles of the devil. For we wrestle not against flesh and blood, but against principalities, against powers, against the rulers of the darkness of this world, against spiritual wickedness in high places. Wherefore take unto you the whole armour of God, that ye may be able to withstand in the evil day, and having done all, to stand.

Ephesians 6:10-13

Christian Citizenship

The Bible teaches both in the Old and New Testament that to be a good citizen is to be a good and religious person. The church has traditionally taught good citizenship as part of being a good Christian. Included in this section are songs of patriotism as well as hymns and songs which are appropriate for national holidays.

THE NATIONAL ANTHEM

Francis Scott Key

John S. Smith

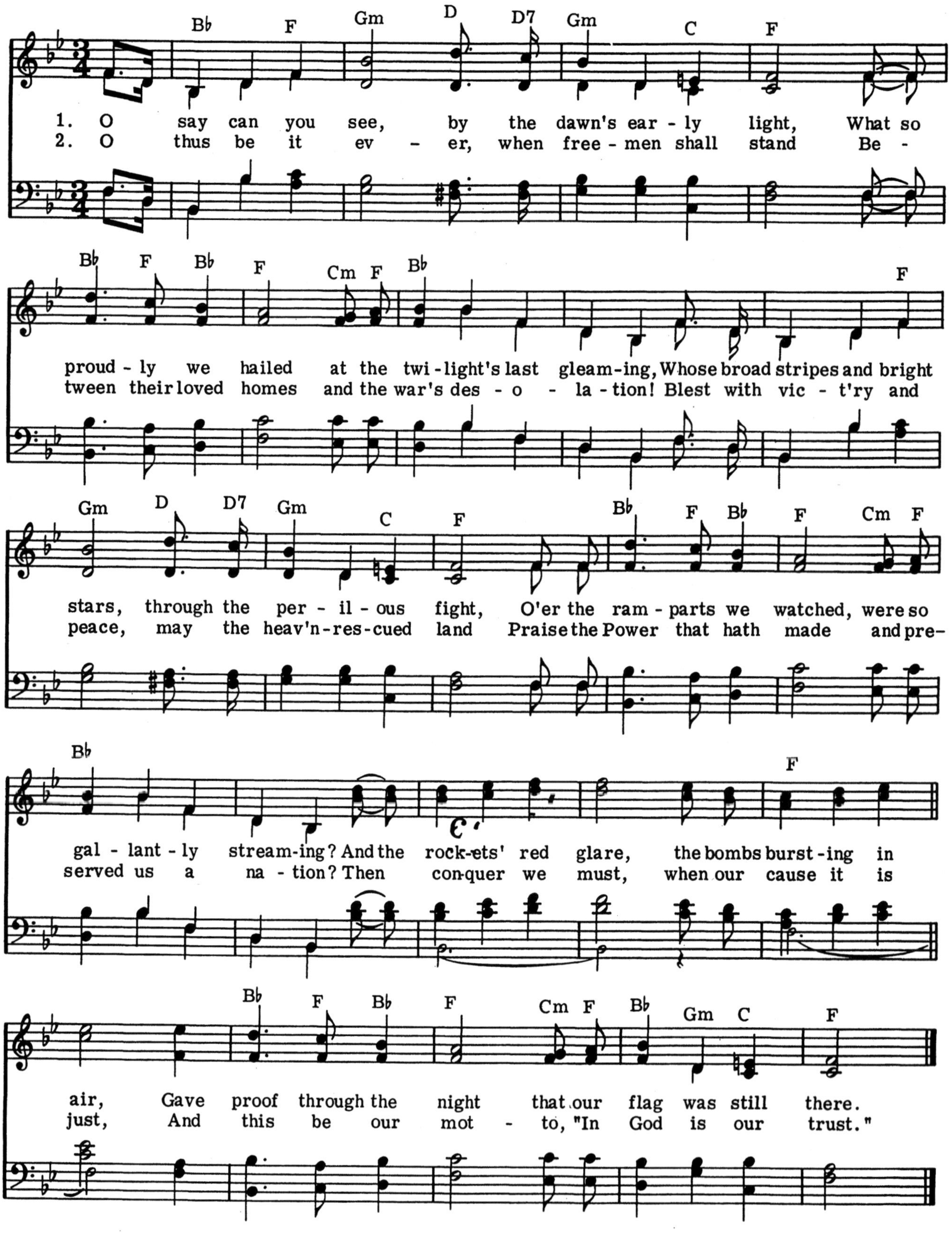

Bb F Gm D D7 Gm C F
1. O say can you see, by the dawn's ear - ly light, What so
2. O thus be it ev - er, when free - men shall stand Be -
Bb F Bb F Cm F Bb F
proud - ly we hailed at the twi - light's last gleam - ing, Whose broad stripes and bright
tween their loved homes and the war's des - o - la - tion! Blest with vic - t'ry and
Gm D D7 Gm C F Bb F Bb F Cm F
stars, through the per - il - ous fight, O'er the ram - parts we watched, were so
peace, may the heav'n - res - cued land Praise the Power that hath made and pre-
Bb F
gal - lant - ly stream - ing? And the rock - ets' red glare, the bombs burst - ing in
served us a na - tion? Then con - quer we must, when our cause it is
Bb F Bb F Cm F Bb Gm C F
air, Gave proof through the night that our flag was still there.
just, And this be our mot - to, "In God is our trust."

MY COUNTRY! 'TIS OF THEE

Samuel Smith   Original Source unknown

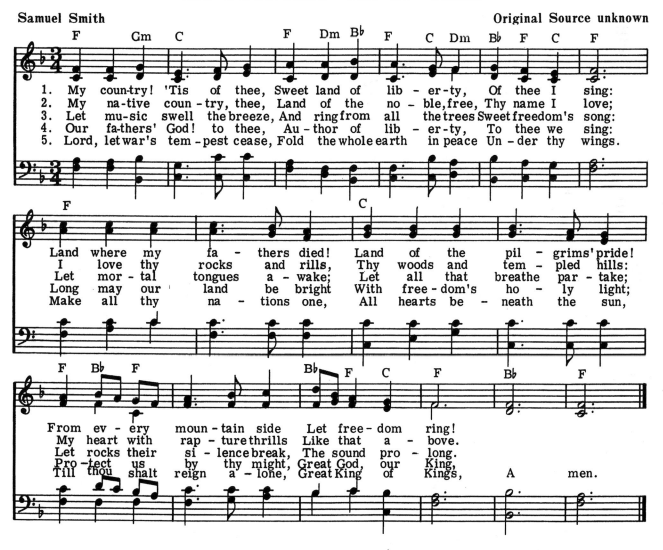

1. My coun-try! 'Tis of thee, Sweet land of lib - er-ty, Of thee I sing:
2. My na-tive coun-try, thee, Land of the no - ble,free, Thy name I love;
3. Let mu-sic swell the breeze, And ring from all the trees Sweet freedom's song:
4. Our fa-thers' God! to thee, Au-thor of lib - er-ty, To thee we sing:
5. Lord, let war's tem-pest cease, Fold the whole earth in peace Un - der thy wings.

Land where my fa - thers died! Land of the pil - grims' pride!
I love thy rocks and rills, Thy woods and tem - pled hills:
Let mor - tal tongues a - wake; Let all that breathe par - take;
Long may our land be bright With free - dom's ho - ly light;
Make all thy na - tions one, All hearts be - neath the sun,

From ev - ery moun-tain side Let free-dom ring!
My heart with rap - ture thrills Like that a - bove.
Let rocks their si - lence break, The sound pro - long.
Pro - tect us by thy might, Great God, our King,
Till thou shalt reign a - lone, Great King of Kings, A men.

HYMN TUNE: AMERICA

95

MINE EYES HAVE SEEN THE GLORY

This tune was written by the Southerner J.W. Staffe in 1855. It became popular throughout the country with several sets of lyrics. Julia Ward Howe, a passionate abolitionist, heard the tune in 1861 as the Civil War was beginning, and was inspired to write this text. The song became associated with President Abraham Lincoln because of his desire to free the slaves and was a rallying call to the Union Army throughout the War.

Julia Ward Howe

American Camp Meeting Tune

1. Mine eyes have seen the glo - ry of the com - ing of the Lord; He is tram - pling out the vin - tage where the grapes of wrath are stored; He hath loosed the fate - ful light - ning of his ter - ri - ble swift sword; His truth is march - ing on.

2. I have seen him in the watch - fires of a hun - dred cir - cling camps; They have build - ed him an al - tar in the eve - ning dews and damps; I can read his right - eous sen - tence by the dim and flar - ing lamps; His day is march - ing on.

3. He has sound - ed forth the trum - pet that shall nev - er call re - treat; He is sift - ing out the hearts of men be - fore his judg - ment seat; O be swift, my soul, to an - swer him; be ju - bi - lant, my feet! Our God is march - ing on.

4. In the beau - ty of the lil - ies Christ was born a - cross the sea, With a glo - ry in his bos - om that trans - fig - ures you and me; As he died to make men ho - ly, let us die to make men free! While God is march - ing on.

5. He is com - ing like the glo - ry of the morn - ing on the wave; He is wis - dom to the might - y, he is hon - or to the brave; So the world shall be his foot - stool, and the soul of wrong his slave. Our God is march - ing on.

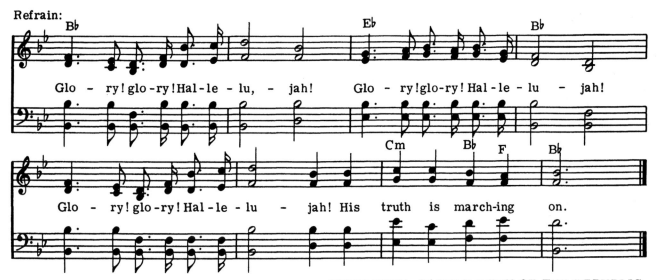

Refrain:

Glo - ry! glo - ry! Hal - le - lu, - jah! Glo - ry! glo - ry! Hal - le - lu - jah!

Glo - ry! glo - ry! Hal - le - lu - jah! His truth is march-ing on.

HYMN TUNE: BATTLE HYMN OF THE REPUBLIC

GOD, THAT MADEST EARTH AND HEAVEN

Heber; Hosmer   Traditional Welsh melody

1. God, that mad-est earth and heav-en, Dark - ness and light;
2. When the con-stant sun re-turn-ing Un - seals our eyes,

Who the day for toil hast giv - en, For rest the night:
May we, born a - new like morn-ing, to la - bor rise;

May thine an - gel guards de - fend us, Slum - ber sweet thy mer - cy send us,
Gird us for the task that call us, Let not ease and self en thrall us,

Ho - ly dreams and hopes at-tend us, This live-long night.
Strong through thee, what - e'er be-fall us, O God most wise! A - men.

HYMN TUNE: AR HYD Y NOS

97

O BEAUTIFUL FOR SPACIOUS SKIES

The poetess Katherine Lee Bates was inspired to write the words after a visit to Pike's Peak in 1893. The tune "Materna" was written by Samuel Ward, the owner of a New Jersey music store and composer of many songs and piano pieces.

Katherine Lee Bates

Samuel A. Ward

1. O beau-ti-ful for spa-cious skies, For am-ber waves of grain,
2. O beau-ti-ful for pil-grim feet, Whose stern, im-pas-sioned stress
3. O beau-ti-ful for he-roes proved In lib-er-a-ting strife,
4. O beau-ti-ful for pa-triot dream That sees, be-yond the years,

For pur-ple moun-tain maj-es-ties A-bove the fruit-ed plain!
A thor-ough-fare for free-dom beat A-cross the wil-der-ness!
Who more than self their coun-try loved, And mer-cy more than life!
Thine al-a-bas-ter cit-ies gleam, Un-dimmed by hu-man tears!

A - mer - i - ca! A - mer - i - ca! God shed his grace on thee,
A - mer - i - ca! A - mer - i - ca! God mend thine ev - ery flaw;
A - mer - i - ca! A - mer - i - ca! May God thy gold re - fine,
A - mer - i - ca! A - mer - i - ca! God shed his grace on thee,

And crown thy good with broth-er-hood From sea to shin-ing sea.
Con-firm thy soul in self-con-trol, Thy lib-er-ty in law.
Till all suc-cess be no-ble-ness, And ev-ery, gain di-vine.
And crown thy good with broth-er-hood From sea to shin-ing sea. A - men.

HYMN TUNE: MATERNA

FAITH OF OUR FATHERS, LIVING STILL

Frederick Faber originally wrote this hymn when he left the Church of England and was converted to Catholicism. The text has since been changed so that "Faith" refers to the teachings of Christ rather than any particular religion. One of the hymn's most important messages is that we must love our enemies and show them a good example, so that they too may be drawn to Christ.

Henri F. Hemy
Adapted by James G. Walton

Frederick Faber

1. Faith of our fa - thers, liv - ing still In spite of dun - geon, fire, and sword! O how our hearts beat high with joy When-e'er we hear that glo - rious word! Faith of our fa - thers, ho - ly faith! We will be true to thee till death.

2. Faith of our fa - thers, God's great power Shall win all na - tions un - to thee, And through the truth that comes from God Man - kind shall then be tru - ly free. Faith of our fa - thers, ho - ly faith! We will be true to thee till death.

3. Faith of our fa - thers, we will love Both friend and foe in all our strife, And preach thee, too, as love knows how By kind - ly words and vir - tuous life: Faith of our fa - thers, ho - ly faith! We will be true to thee till death. A - men.

HYMN TUNE: ST. CATHERINE

COME, YE THANKFUL PEOPLE, COME

Henry Alford was the Dean at Canterbury Cathedral in England when this text was written to celebrate the English Harvest Festival. Now, of course, this hymn has become a favorite for use in the United States at Thanksgiving. The fourth verse has a missions emphasis and speaks of the world as a field "ripe for harvest". "St. George's Windsor" was composed by George Elvey who was organist at St. George's Chapel, Windsor, for forty-seven years.

Henry Alford   George Elvey

HYMN TUNE: ST. GEORGE'S WINDSOR

WE GATHER TOGETHER TO ASK THE LORD'S BLESSING

This hymn is popular for use during the Thanksgiving season as it expresses our gratefulness to God for his watchful care over us.

Sixteenth century Dutch hymn
Theodore Baker, Tr.

Arr. by Edward Kremser

1. We gath - er to geth - er to ask the Lord's bless - ing;
2. Be - side us to guide us, our God with us join - ing,
3. We all do ex - tol thee, thou Lead - er tri - um - phant,

He chas - tens and has - tens, his will to make known
Or - dain - ing, main - tain - ing his king - dom di - vine;
And pray that thou still our de - fend - er wilt be.

The wick - ed op - press - ing now cease from dis - tress - ing,
So from the be - gin - ning the fight we were win - ning:
Let thy con - gre - ga - tion es - cape trib - u - la - tion:

Sing prais - es to his name; he for-gets not his own.
Thou, Lord, wast at our side, all glo - ry be thine!
Thy name be ev - er praised! O Lord, make us free! A - men.

HYMN TUNE: KREMSER

NOW THANK WE ALL OUR GOD

Martin Rinckaert was a German writer and poet who wrote this text during the Thirty Years War. It is rather remarkable that a man who faced death daily as he did, was still able to offer thanks and praise to God who stood stronger than the horrors of war. This hymn has been used for many important occasions because of its triumphant message. The stately tune by Johann Crüger along with other similar chorales became an integral part of the hymns used in the Lutheran Church.

Martin Rinckaert

Johann Crüger

1. Now thank we all our God With hearts and hands and voic - es,
2. O may this boun-teous God Through all our life be near - us,
3. All praise and thanks to God The Fa-ther now be giv - en,

Who won-drous things hath done, In whom his world re - joic - es;
With ev - er joy-ful hearts And bless-ed peace to cheer - us;
The Son, and him who reigns With them in high-est heav - en,

Who, from our moth-ers' arms, Hath blessed us on our way
And keep us in his grace, And guide us when per - plexed,
The one e - ter - nal God, Whom earth and heaven a - dore;

With count-less gifts of love, And still is ours to - day.
And free us from all ills In this world and the next.
For thus it was, is now, And shall be ev - er - more. A - men.

HYMN TUNE: NUN DANKET

Songs
for Young People

Perhaps the single most important group in the Christian Church is the group which we label children and/or young people. The future of the Church rests with them, and their Christian education both through scripture and song cannot be overemphasized. Even the two and three year old is capable of learning songs which will explain who Jesus is and the tremendous love which He has for each of us. These songs are both for young people and/or about young people and are meant to be used by a variety of age groups. It is hoped that their message will be meaningful!

SING YE AND SHOUT

Pamela C. Bye

Pamela C. Bye

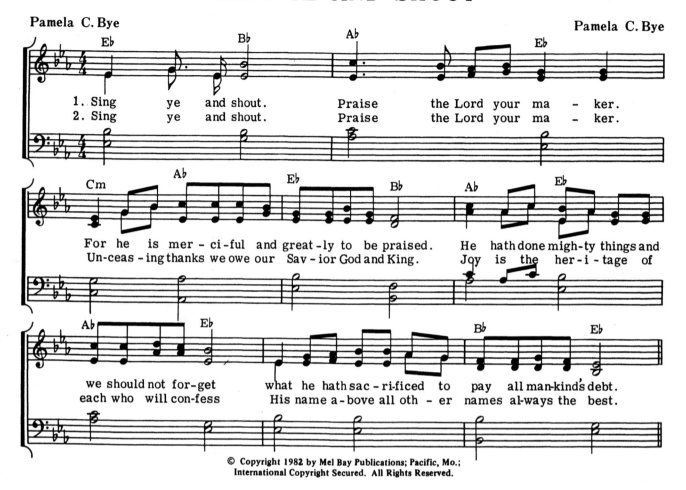

1. Sing ye and shout. Praise the Lord your ma - ker.
2. Sing ye and shout. Praise the Lord your ma - ker.

For he is mer - ci - ful and great - ly to be praised. He hath done migh - ty things and
Un - ceas - ing thanks we owe our Sav - ior God and King. Joy is the her - i - tage of

we should not for - get what he hath sac - ri - ficed to pay all man - kind's debt.
each who will con - fess His name a - bove all oth - er names al - ways the best.

PRAISE HIM, ALL YE LITTLE CHILDREN

Anonymous

Anonymous

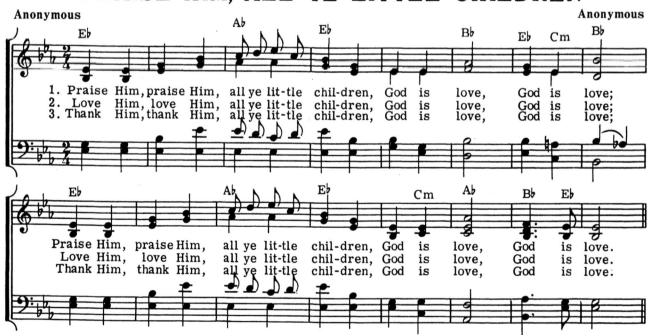

1. Praise Him, praise Him, all ye lit - tle chil - dren, God is love, God is love;
2. Love Him, love Him, all ye lit - tle chil - dren, God is love, God is love;
3. Thank Him, thank Him, all ye lit - tle chil - dren, God is love, God is love;

Praise Him, praise Him, all ye lit - tle chil - dren, God is love, God is love.
Love Him, love Him, all ye lit - tle chil - dren, God is love, God is love.
Thank Him, thank Him, all ye lit - tle chil - dren, God is love, God is love:

HYMN TUNE: GOD IS LOVE

SUFFER THE LITTLE CHILDREN

Pamela C. Bye   Pamela C. Bye

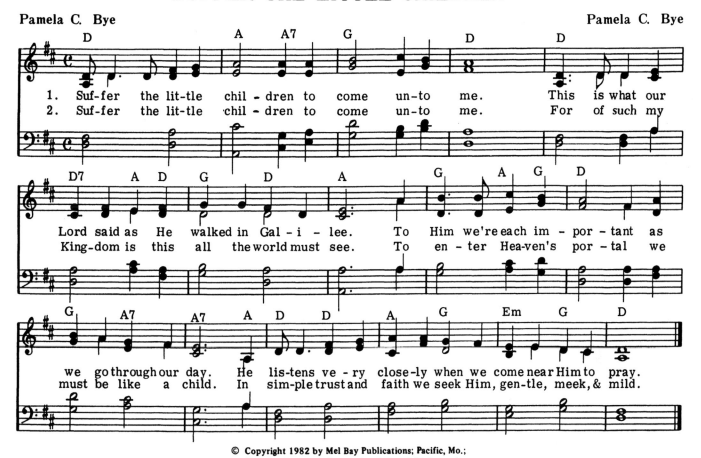

1. Suf-fer the lit-tle chil-dren to come un-to me. This is what our
2. Suf-fer the lit-tle chil-dren to come un-to me. For of such my

Lord said as He walked in Gal-i-lee. To Him we're each im-por-tant as
King-dom is this all the world must see. To en-ter Hea-ven's por-tal we

we go through our day. He lis-tens ve-ry close-ly when we come near Him to pray.
must be like a child. In sim-ple trust and faith we seek Him, gen-tle, meek, & mild.

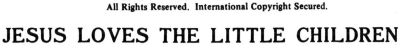

JESUS LOVES THE LITTLE CHILDREN

C. H. Woolston   George F. Root

Je - sus loves the lit - tle chil - dren, All the chil-dren of the

world; red and yel - low black and white, They are pre - cious in his

sight, Je - sus loves the lit - tle chil - dren of the world.

ALL THINGS BRIGHT AND BEAUTIFUL

Frances Alexander was a well-respected Irish hymn writer whose special talent was in her writing of children's hymns. The inspiration for this particular text came from the Apostles' Creed; especially the phrase, "Maker of Heaven and earth". This tune is just one of many which has been used with the text, but whatever tune is used, the hymn is a favorite of all ages.

Cecil Frances Alexander

W. R. Waghorne

1. All things bright and beau - ti - ful, All crea - tures great and small,
All things wise and won - der - ful, The Lord God made them all.

2. Each lit - tle, flow'r that o - pens, Each lit - tle bird that sings,
3. The cold wind in the win - ter, The pleas - ant sum - mer sun,
4. The tall trees in the green - wood, The mead - ows where we play,
5. He gave us eyes to see them, And lips that we might tell

He made their glow - ing col - ors, He made their ti - ny wings.
The ripe fruits in the gar - den, He made them ev - 'ry one.
The rush - es by the wa - ter We gath - er ev - 'ry day;
How great is God Al - might - y, Who has made all things well.

BEAUTIFUL SAVIOR

This hymn, because of its many references to nature, is a favorite of children who closely identify with the things around them. One of the first ways of explaining God to children is usually through examples of creation; trees, flowers, animals, and finally we ourselves.

Joseph A. Seiss   Silesian Folk tune

1. Beau - ti - ful Sav - ior, King of cre - a - tion,
2. Fair are the mead - ows, fair are the wood - lands,

Son of God and Son of Man!
robed in flow'rs of bloom - ing spring;

Tru - ly I'd love thee, tru - ly I'd serve thee,
Je - sus is fair - er, Je - sus is pur - er,

Light of my soul, my joy, my crown.
He makes our sor - rowing spir - it sing.

* Guitar: Capo on 1st, play in D

ALL PRAISE TO THEE, MY GOD, THIS NIGHT

Thomas Ken

Thomas Tallis

1. All praise to thee, my God, this night, For all the bless-ings of the light!
2. For - give me, Lord, for thy dear Son, The ill that I this day have done;
3. O may my soul on thee re-pose, And with sweet sleep mine eye - lids close;
4. Praise God from whom all bless-ings flow; Praise him, all crea-tures here be - low;

Keep me, O keep me, King of kings, Be - neath thine own al-might-y wings.
That with the world, my - self, and thee, I, ere I sleep, at peace may be.
Sleep that may me more vig-orous make To serve my God when I a-wake.
Praise him a-bove, ye heaven-ly host; Praise Fa-ther, Son, and Ho - ly Ghost. A - men.

(This is a canon. The melody begins at *)

HYMN TUNE: TALLIS CANON

NOW THE DAY IS OVER

Sabine Baring-Gould

Joseph Barnby

1. Now the day is o - ver, Night is draw-ing nigh,
2. Je - sus, give the wea - ry Calm and sweet re - pose;

Sha - dows of the eve - ning Steal a-cross the sky.
With thy ten d'rest bless - ing May our eye-lids close. A - men.

eve-ning Steal a - cross the sky.
bless-ing May our eye - - lids close.

HYMN TUNE: MERRIAL

108

DONA NOBIS PACEM
(THIS MAY BE SUNG AS A ROUND)

These Latin words which mean "Grant us peace", make up one of the most popular of the religious rounds. This short text is nevertheless one of the most fervent prayers and strongest beliefs of the Christian Church.

JACOB'S LADDER

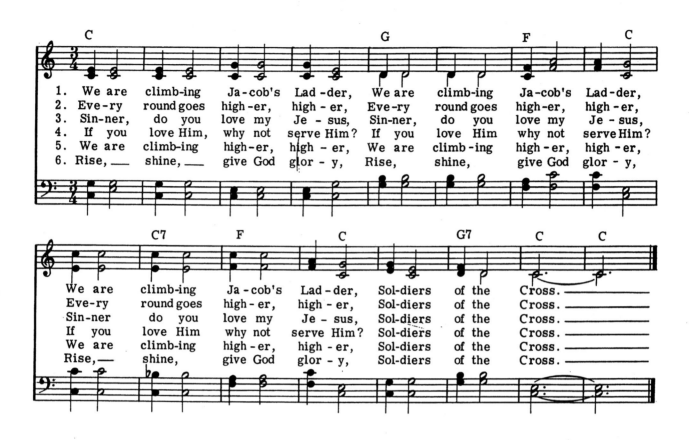

1. We are climb-ing Ja-cob's Lad-der, We are climb-ing Ja-cob's Lad-der,
2. Eve-ry round goes high-er, high-er, Eve-ry round goes high-er, high-er,
3. Sin-ner, do you love my Je-sus, Sin-ner, do you love my Je-sus,
4. If you love Him, why not serve Him? If you love Him why not serve Him?
5. We are climb-ing high-er, high-er, We are climb-ing high-er, high-er,
6. Rise,— shine,— give God glor-y, Rise, shine, give God glor-y,

We are climb-ing Ja-cob's Lad-der, Sol-diers of the Cross.
Eve-ry round goes high-er, high-er, Sol-diers of the Cross.
Sin-ner do you love my Je-sus, Sol-diers of the Cross.
If you love Him why not serve Him? Sol-diers of the Cross.
We are climb-ing high-er, high-er, Sol-diers of the Cross.
Rise,— shine, give God glor-y, Sol-diers of the Cross.

KUM BA YAH

(COME BY HERE)

African Spiritual

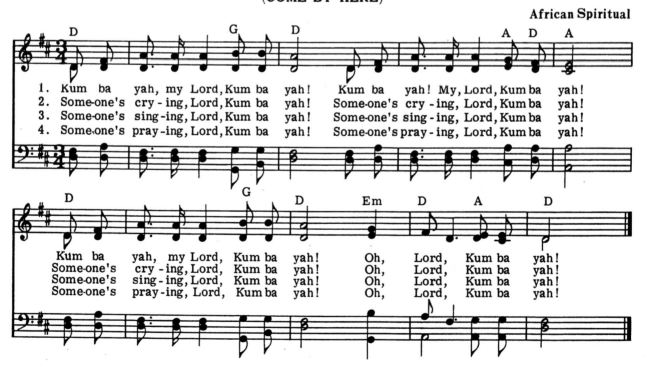

1. Kum ba yah, my Lord, Kum ba yah! Kum ba yah! My, Lord, Kum ba yah!
2. Some-one's cry-ing, Lord, Kum ba yah! Some-one's cry-ing, Lord, Kum ba yah!
3. Some-one's sing-ing, Lord, Kum ba yah! Some-one's sing-ing, Lord, Kum ba yah!
4. Some-one's pray-ing, Lord, Kum ba yah! Some-one's pray-ing, Lord, Kum ba yah!

Kum ba yah, my Lord, Kum ba yah! Oh, Lord, Kum ba yah!
Some-one's cry-ing, Lord, Kum ba yah! Oh, Lord, Kum ba yah!
Some-one's sing-ing, Lord, Kum ba yah! Oh, Lord, Kum ba yah!
Some-one's pray-ing, Lord, Kum ba yah! Oh, Lord, Kum ba yah!

JESUS LOVES ME

This is one of the most widely sung children's songs and is probably the first one a child learns in church. William Bradbury, composer of the tune, organized singing classes in New York City where he was organist at the First Baptist Church. These classes have been credited with the introduction of music into the public schools. Bradbury wrote fifty-nine singing books. His belief that <u>everyone</u> should sing, pervaded his work until his death in 1868.

Anna B. Warner

William Bradbury

1. Je-sus loves me! this I know, For the Bi-ble tells me so;
2. Je-sus loves me! He who died Heav-en's gates to o-pen wide!
3. Je-sus loves me! loves me still, Tho' I'm ver-y weak and ill;
4. Je-sus loves me! He will stay Close be-side me all the way;

Lit-tle ones to Him be-long; They are weak, but He is strong.
He will wash a-way my sin, Let His lit-tle child come in.
From His shin-ing throne on high, Comes to watch me where I lie.
If I love Him, when I die He will take me home on high.

REFRAIN

Yes, Je-sus loves me, Yes, Je-sus loves me,

Yes, Je-sus loves me, The Bi-ble tells me so.

HYMN TUNE: CHINA

THERE WERE TWELVE DISCIPLES

This is an excellent way for children and youth to remember the names of the twelve disciples, and to sing the message that the call didn't stop with them, but that all "present day" Christians are called as well.

Anon.

George A. Minor

There were twelve dis-ci-ples Je-sus called to help Him: Si-mon Pe-ter, An-drew, James, his bro-ther John; Phil-ip, Thom-as, Mat-thew, James, the son of Al-pheus, Thad-deus, Si-mon, Ju-das, And Bar-thol-o-mew.

CHORUS

He has called us too, He has called us too; We are His dis-ci-

1. ples, I am one and you.

2. ples, We His work must do.

112

ZACCHAEUS

This text is taken from the nineteenth chapter of Luke which relates the story of Zacchaeus' struggle to see Jesus. Children love to sing this with hand motions. They, of course, can easily understand the difficulty someone small might have in a large crowd!

① Zac - chae-us was a wee lit-tle man, a wee lit-tle man was he. ② He climbed up in a syc-a-more tree for the Lord he want-ed to see. And as the Sav-ior passed that way, he looked up in the tree; and he said: "Zacchaeus, come on down, for I'm going to your house to - day, for I'm go-ing to your house to - day."

1. Hands in front, right palm above left palm. 2. Palms closer together. 3. Climbing motion with hands. 4. Shade eyes with hand and look down. 5. Shade eyes with hand and look up. 6. Speak these words. 7. Clap on accented beats.

And behold there was a man named Zacchaeus, which was the chief among the publicans, and he was rich. And he sought to see Jesus who he was, and could not for the press because he was little of stature. And he ran before and climbed up into a sycamore tree to see him: for he was to pass that way. And when Jesus came to the place, he looked up and saw him, and said unto him, Zacchaeus, make haste, and come down; for today I must abide at thy house.

Luke 19:2-5

IF I WERE A BUTTERFLY

Brian Howard   Brian Howard

1. If I were a but-ter-fly, I'd thank you Lord for giv-ing me wings, and
2. If I were an el-e-phant, I'd thank you Lord by rais-ing my trunk, and
3. If I were a wigg-ly worm, I'd thank you Lord that I ___ could squirm, and

If I were a ro-bin in a tree, I'd thank you Lord that I could sing, and
If I were a kan-ga-roo, I'd hop, hop, hop, right up to you, and
If I were a fuzzy wuzzy bear, I'd thank you Lord for my fuzzy wuzzy hair, and

If I were a fish in the sea, I'd wig-gle my tail and gig-gle with glee, but
If I were an oc-ta-pus, I'd thank you Lord for my fine looks, but
If I were a cro-co-dile, I'd thank you Lord for my big smile, but

I just thank you Fa-ther for mak-ing me me. Be-cause you
I just thank you Fa-ther for mak-ing me me.
I just thank you Fa-ther for mak-ing me me.

Chorus

114

gave me a heart, you gave me a smile, You gave me Lord Je-sus and you

made me His child, But I just thank you Fa-ther for mak-ing me me.

HE'S GOT THE WHOLE WORLD IN HIS HANDS

Spiritual   Spiritual

1. He's got the whole _____ world _____ in his hands,_ he's got the
2. He's got the ti - ny lit - tle ba - by_ in his hands,_ he's got the
3. He's got _____ you and me _____ broth-er_ in his hands,_ he's got _____
4. He's got _____ ev - 'ry - bod - y _____ in his hands,_ he's got _____

whole _____ world _____ in his hands, he's got the whole _____ world _____
ti - ny lit - tle ba-by_ in his hands, he's got the ti - ny lit -tle ba - by_
you and me _____ sis-ter_ in his hands, he's got _____ you and me _____ broth-er_
ev - 'ry _____ bod-y _____ in his hands, he's got _____ ev - 'ry _____ bod-y _____

in his hands,_ he's got the whole world in his_ hands.
in his hands,_ he's got the whole world in his_ hands.
in his hands,_ he's got the whole world in his_ hands.
in his hands,_ he's got the whole world in his_ hands.

OH, BE CAREFUL

Anonymous

Old Melody

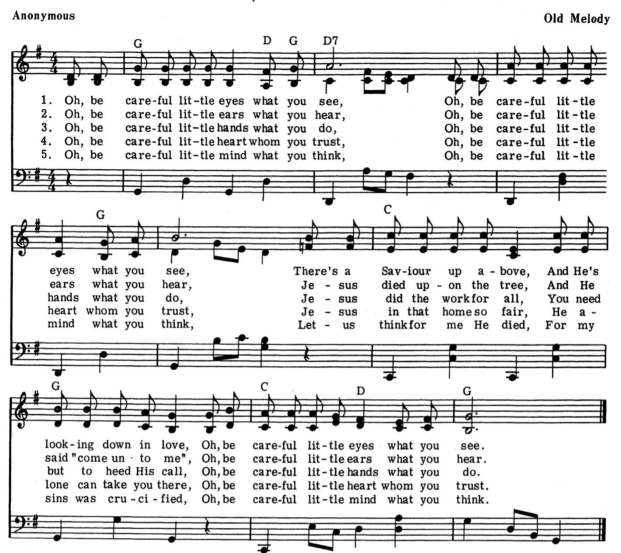

1. Oh, be care-ful lit-tle eyes what you see, Oh, be care-ful lit-tle eyes what you see, There's a Sav-iour up a-bove, And He's look-ing down in love, Oh, be care-ful lit-tle eyes what you see.

2. Oh, be care-ful lit-tle ears what you hear, Oh, be care-ful lit-tle ears what you hear, Je-sus died up-on the tree, And He said "come un-to me", Oh, be care-ful lit-tle ears what you hear.

3. Oh, be care-ful lit-tle hands what you do, Oh, be care-ful lit-tle hands what you do, Je-sus did the work for all, You need but to heed His call, Oh, be care-ful lit-tle hands what you do.

4. Oh, be care-ful lit-tle heart whom you trust, Oh, be care-ful lit-tle heart whom you trust, Je-sus in that home so fair, He a-lone can take you there, Oh, be care-ful lit-tle heart whom you trust.

5. Oh, be care-ful lit-tle mind what you think, Oh, be care-ful lit-tle mind what you think, Let-us think for me He died, For my sins was cru-ci-fied, Oh, be care-ful lit-tle mind what you think.

Vs.6 Oh, be careful little tongue what you say
Vs.7 Oh, be careful little feet where you go

FOR HEALTH AND STRENGTH

It is of utmost importance to teach children that they should give God thanks for all they have. An appropriate way to do this is before each meal. This little prayer song is a favorite with children, and its message is very clear.

Unknown

Unknown

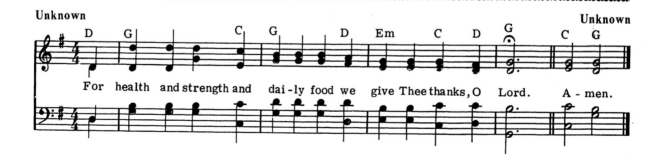

For health and strength and dai-ly food we give Thee thanks, O Lord. A-men.

The Christmas Season

The carol dates back to the fifteenth century, and it became popular along with the ballad because the people wanted something more vivacious and less severe than the old Latin hymns they had been singing. The Christmas season, along with the accompanying seasons of Advent and Epiphany, is perhaps the most joyous time of the Christian year. It is difficult to choose a favorite carol because each has its own special beauty, so an effort has been made to include a variety both by country of origin and period of history.

OF THE FATHER'S LOVE BEGOTTEN

Aurelius Prudentius

13th Century Plainsong

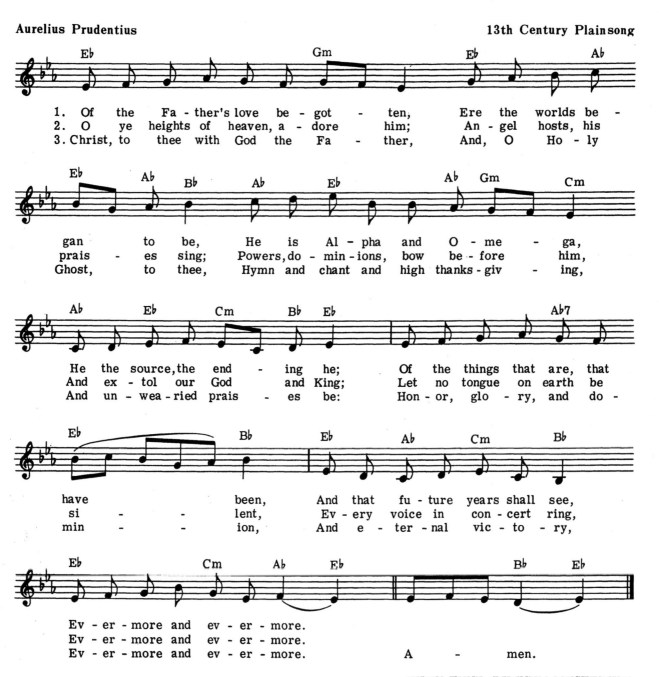

HYMN TUNE: DIVINUM MYSTERIUM

I am Alpha and Omega, the beginning and the ending, saith the Lord, which is, and which was, and which is to come, the Almighty.

Revelation 1:8

And he said unto me, It is done. I am Alpha and Omega, the beginning and the end. I will give unto him that is athirst of the fountain of the water of life freely.

Revelation 21:6

COME, THOU LONG-EXPECTED JESUS

Charles Wesley

Rowland Prichard

1. Come, thou long – ex – pec – ted Je – sus, Born to set thy
2. Born thy peo – ple to de – liv – er, Born a child and

peo – ple free; From our fears and sins re – lease us!
yet a king, Born to reign in us for – ev – er,

Let us find our rest in thee. Is – rael's strength and con – so –
Now thy gra – cious king – dom bring! By thine own e – ter – nal

la – tion, Hope of all the earth thou art; Dear de – sire of
Spir – it Rule in all our hearts a – lone; By thine all – suf –

ev – ery na – tion, Joy of ev – ery long – ing heart.
fic – ient mer – it Raise us to thy glo – rious throne! A – men.

HYMN TUNE: HYFRYDOL

119

BREAK FORTH, O BEAUTEOUS HEAV'NLY LIGHT

The text of this glorious hymn is based on Isaiah 9: 2-7. The hymn tune was composed by Johann Schop and was harmonized in its present form by J.S. Bach in his "Christmas Oratorio".

ANGELS WE HAVE HEARD ON HIGH

This French carol with its "angelic refrain" probably dates from the eighteenth century. The present arrangement of the hymn tune "Gloria" was made by Edward S. Barnes.

Trad. French – English carol

Trad. Carol

1. An-gels we have heard on high, Sweet-ly sing-ing o'er the plains;
2. Shep-herds, why this ju - bi - lee? Why your joy - ous strains pro - long?
3. Come to Beth - le - hem, and see Him whose birth the an - gels sing;
4. See him in a man-ger laid, Whom the choirs of an - gels praise;

And the moun-tains in re - ply, Ech - o - ing their joy - ous strains.
What the glad-some tid - ings be Which in - spire your heaven-ly song?
Come, a - dore on bend - ed knee Christ the Lord, the new – born King.
Mar - y Jo - seph, lend your aid, While our hearts in love we raise.

Glo - - - - - - - ri-a in ex-cel-sis De o,

Glo - - - - - - - ri-a in ex-cel-sis De o.

HYMN TUNE: GLORIA

121

GOD REST YOU MERRY, GENTLEMEN

18th century English carol

Traditional English carol

1. God rest you merry, gentlemen, Let nothing you dismay,
2. In Bethlehem in Jewry This blessed babe was born,
3. From God our heavenly Father A blessed angel came,
4. The shepherds at those tidings Rejoiced much in mind,
5. Now to the Lord sing praises, All you within this place,

For Jesus Christ our Savior Was born upon this day,
And laid within a manger Upon this blessed morn:
And unto certain shepherds Brought tidings of the same,
And left their flocks a-feeding In tempest, storm, and wind,
And with true love and brotherhood Each other now embrace;

To save us all from Satan's power When we were gone astray.
The which his mother Mary Did nothing take in scorn.
How that in Bethlehem was born The Son of God by name.
And went to Bethlehem straightway, The blessed babe to find.
This holy tide of Christmas All other doth deface.

Refrain

O tidings of comfort and joy, comfort and joy; O tidings of comfort and joy!

HYMN TUNE: GOD REST YOU MERRY

122

O LITTLE TOWN OF BETHLEHEM

This hymn text was written by one of America's most distinguished preachers, Bishop Phillips Brooks of Massachusetts. Lewis Redner, who wrote the hymn tune "St. Louis", was the organist at Holy Trinity Church in Philadelphia while Brooks was the minister. The beauty of this hymn lies mainly in the simplicity of its message of the birth of Jesus.

Phillips Brooks

Lewis H. Redner

1. O little town of Bethlehem, How still we see thee lie! Above thy deep and dream-less sleep The silent stars go by; Yet in thy dark streets shineth The ev-er-last-ing Light; The hopes and fears of all the years Are met in thee to-night.

2. For Christ is born of Mary, And, gath-ered all a-bove While mor-tals sleep, the an-gels keep Their watch of won-dering love. O morn-ing stars, to-geth-er Pro-claim the ho-ly birth, And prais-es sing to God the King, And peace to men on earth!

3. How si-lent-ly, how si-lent-ly The won-drous gift is given! So God im-parts to hu-man hearts The bless-ings of his heaven. No ear may hear his com-ing, But in this world of sin, Where meek souls will re-ceive him, still The dear Christ en-ters in.

4. O ho-ly Child of Bethlehem! De-scend to us, we pray; Cast out our sin and en-ter in; Be born in us to-day. We hear the Christ-mas an-gels The great glad tid-ings tell; O come to us, a-bide with us, Our Lord Im-man-u-el! A-men.

HYMN TUNE: ST. LOUIS

THE FIRST NOEL

Traditional English carol

English Folk song

1. The first no - el, the an - gel did say, Was to
2. They look - ed up and saw a star Shin-ing
3. And by the light of that same star Three
4. This star drew nigh to the north - west; O'er
5. Then en - tered in those wise men three, Full

cer - tain poor shep-herds in fields as they lay, In fields where
in the east, be - yond them far, And to the
wise men came from coun - try far; To seek for a
Beth - le - hem it took its rest, And there it
rev - er - ent - ly up - on the knee, And of - fered

they lay keep - ing their sheep On a cold win - ter's
earth it gave great light, And so it con -
king was their in - tent, And to fol - low the
did both stop and stay, Right o - ver the
there, in his pres - ence Their gold and

night that was so deep. *REFRAIN* No - el, No - el, No -
tin - ued both day and night.
star wher - ev - er it went.
place where Je - sus lay.
myrrh and frank - in - cense.

el, No - el, Born is the king of Is - ra - el.

HYMN TUNE : THE FIRST NOEL

124

AWAY IN A MANGER

Vs. 3 John McFarland

James R. Murray

1. A - way in a man - ger, no crib for a bed,
2. The cat - tle are low - ing, the ba - by a - wakes,
3. Be near me, Lord Je - sus, I ask thee to stay

The lit - tle Lord Je - sus laid down his sweet head.
But lit - tle Lord Je - sus, no cry - ing he makes.
Close by me for - ev - er, and love me, I pray.

The stars in the sky looked down where he lay,
I love thee, Lord Je - sus, look down from the sky,
Bless all the dear chil - dren in thy ten - der care,

The lit - tle Lord Je - sus, a - sleep on the hay.
And stay by my cra - dle till morn-ing is nigh.
And fit us for heav-en to live with thee there. A - men.

HYMN TUNE: AWAY IN A MANGER

And she brought forth her firstborn son, and wrapped him in swaddling clothes, and laid him in a manger; because there was no room for them in the inn.

Luke 2:7

WHAT CHILD IS THIS

William Dix was not by profession a musician, but he wrote many original hymns which have become popular. This text stresses the simplicity of Jesus' birth while expressing the honor due Him as Christ, the King. The hymn tune "Greensleeves" has been very popular from its earliest mention in England in the 1500's. It also has the distinction of being referred to twice by the famous playwright William Shakespeare.

William C. Dix

Old English melody

1. What child is this who, laid to rest, On Mary's lap is sleep - ing?
2. Why lies he in such mean es - tate Where ox and ass are feed - ing?
3. So bring him in - cense, gold, and myrrh; Come, peas - ant, king, to own him;

Whom an - gels greet with an - thems sweet, While shep-herds watch are keep - ing?
Good Chris - tian, fear: For sin - ners here The si lent Word is plead - ing.
The King of kings sal - va - tion brings. Let lov - ing hearts en - throne him!

REFRAIN Unison or Harmony

This, this is Christ the King, Whom shep-herds guard and an - gels sing:

Haste, haste to bring him laud, The Babe, the Son of Ma - ry. A - men.

HYMN TUNE: GREENSLEEVES

126

O COME, ALL YE FAITHFUL

This great carol of praise "Adeste Fideles" was originally written in Latin by John F. Wade in the mid eighteenth century. It was translated into English in 1841 by Frederick Oakeley and has since become one of the most popular of all Christmas carols. It tells of the joy all Christians feel at Christ's birth and speaks of the fulfillment of God's promise in the Old Testament.

John F. Wade

Wade's "Cantus Diversi"

1. O come, all ye faith - ful, joy - ful and tri - um - phant,
2. Sing, choirs of an - gels, sing in ex - ul - ta - tion,
3. Yea, Lord, we greet thee, born this hap - py morn - ing,

O come ye, O come ye to Beth - le - hem! Come and be - hold him,
Sing, all ye cit - i - zens of heaven a - bove! Glo - ry to God, all
Je - sus, to thee be all glo - ry given; Word of the Fa - ther,

born the King of an - gels! O come, let us a - dore him, O come, let us a -
glo - ry in the high - est!
now in flesh ap - pear - ing!

REFRAIN

dore him, O come, let us a - dore him, Christ, the Lord! A - men.

HYMN TUNE : ADESTE FIDELES

HARK! THE HERALD ANGELS SING

This is one of the most widely-sung Christmas carols ever written. The text is by Charles Wesley and was written in 1738 at a time when he had been banned from the Church of England because of his emotional brand of religion. By mistake, the verse was included in the Anglican Book of Common Prayer, and even though church leaders objected, it was left because of its popularity with the church members. The tune is from one of the choruses in Mendelssohn's opera "The Festgesang".

Charles Wesley

Mendelssohn - Bartholdy

1. Hark! The her - ald an - gels sing, "Glo - ry to the new-born King;
2. Christ, by high - est heaven a - dored; Christ the ev - er - last - ing Lord!
3. Hail the heaven-born Prince of Peace! Hail the Sun of Right-eous-ness!

Peace on earth, and mer - cy mild; God and sin - ners rec - on - ciled!"
Long de - sired, be - hold him come, Find-ing here his hum - ble home.
Light and life to all he brings, Risen with heal - ing in his wings.

Joy - ful, all ye na - tion, rise; Join the tri - umph of the skies;
Veiled in flesh the God-head see; Hail the in-car-nate De - i - ty,
Mild he lays his glo - ry by, Born that man no more may die,

With an - gel - ic hosts pro-claim, "Christ is born in Beth - le - hem!"
Pleased as man with men to dwell, Je - sus our Em - man - u - el.
Born to raise the sons of earth, Born to give them sec-ond birth.

Refrain

Hark! The her-ald an-gels sing, "Glo-ry to the new-born King." A - men.

HYMN TUNE: MENDELSSOHN

128

GOOD CHRISTIAN MEN, REJOICE

The earliest record of this text appears in about 1400 in Germany. John Mason Neale, the great British writer, included it in his Carols for Christmastide in 1853.

John Mason Neale, tr.

Fourteenth c. German melody

1. Good Chris-tian men, re-joice With heart and soul and voice!
2. Good Chris-tian men, re-joice With heart and soul and voice!
3. Good Chris-tian men, re-joice With heart and soul and voice!

Give ye heed to what we say: News! News! Je-sus Christ is born to-day.
Now ye hear of end-less bliss: Joy! Joy! Je-sus Christ was born for this.
Now ye need not fear the grave: Peace! Peace! Je-sus Christ was born to save;

Man and beast be-fore him bow, And he is in the man-ger now:
He hath oped the heaven-ly door, And man is blessed for ev-er-more.
Calls you one and calls you all, To gain his ev-er-last-ing hall.

Christ is born to-day, Christ is born to-day!
Christ was born for this, Christ was born for this!
Christ was born to save, Christ was born to save! A-men.

HYMN TUNE: IN DULCI JUBILO

JOY TO THE WORLD

This text by Isaac Watts is based on Psalm 98. The tune was arranged by Lowell Mason, the American music educator, and is based on the works of George Frederick Handel.

Isaac Watts

Arr. by Lowell Mason
from works of George F. Handel

1. Joy to the world! The Lord is come: Let earth re-
2. Joy to the world! The Sav - ior reigns: Let men their
3. He rules the world! with truth and grace, And makes the

ceive her King; Let ev - ery heart pre - pare him room,
songs em - ploy While fields and floods, rocks, hills, and plains
na - tions prove The glo - ries of his right - eous - ness,

And heaven and na - ture sing, And heaven and na - ture
Re - peat the sound - ing joy, Re - peat the sound - ing
And won - ders of his love, And won - ders of his

And heaven and na - ture sing,
Re - peat the sound - ing joy,
And won - ders of his love,

And
Re -
And

sing, And heaven, and heaven and na - ture sing.
joy, Re - peat, re - peat the sound - ing joy.
love, And won - ders, won - ders of his love. A - men.

heaven and na - ture sing, and
peat the sound - ing joy, re
won - ders of his love, and

HYMN TUNE: ANTIOCH

130

SILENT NIGHT, HOLY NIGHT

Perhaps no other song holds the hearts of millions in every land as does "Silent Night". The simplicity of its text lends itself easily to translation, so on Christmas Eve it would likely be heard on every continent. The history of the carol has been widely repeated, but the story remains fascinating. Father Joseph Mohr, priest of St. Nicholas Church in Oberndorf, Austria, was distressed because it was Christmas Eve, and the church organ was broken. As he took a quiet walk trying to decide what to do, the words of "Silent Night" came to him. His organist, Franz Gruber, set the text to music, and the carol is probably the most widely-sung of all carols.

Joseph Mohr   Franz Gruber

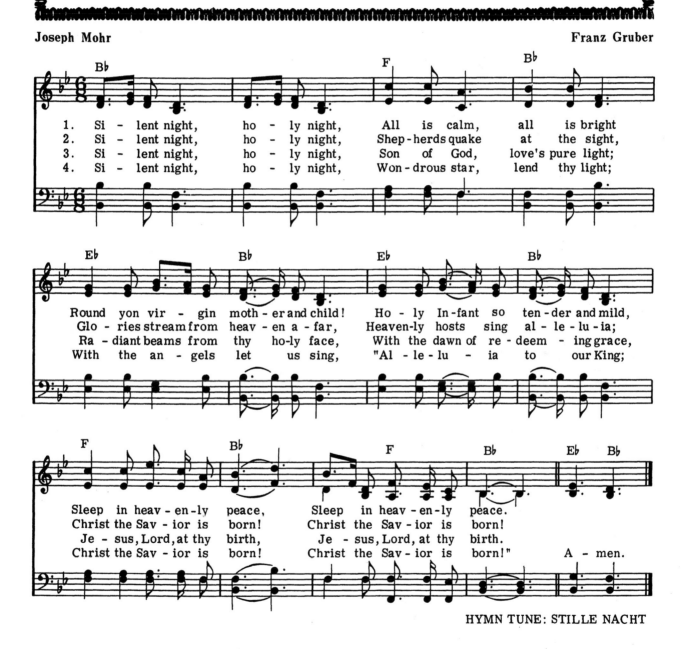

1. Si - lent night, ho - ly night, All is calm, all is bright
2. Si - lent night, ho - ly night, Shep - herds quake at the sight,
3. Si - lent night, ho - ly night, Son of God, love's pure light;
4. Si - lent night, ho - ly night, Won - drous star, lend thy light;

Round yon vir - gin moth - er and child! Ho - ly In-fant so ten - der and mild,
Glo - ries stream from heav - en a - far, Heaven-ly hosts sing al - le - lu - ia;
Ra - diant beams from thy ho-ly face, With the dawn of re - deem - ing grace,
With the an - gels let us sing, "Al - le - lu - ia to our King;

Sleep in heav - en-ly peace, Sleep in heav - en-ly peace.
Christ the Sav - ior is born! Christ the Sav - ior is born!
Je - sus, Lord, at thy birth, Je - sus, Lord, at thy birth.
Christ the Sav - ior is born! Christ the Sav - ior is born!" A - men.

HYMN TUNE: STILLE NACHT

WHILE BY MY SHEEP

Old German text

Seventeenth century carol

1. While by my sheep I watched at night, Glad tidings
2. There shall be born, so he did say, In Bethle-
3. There shall the Child lie in a stall, This Child who
4. This gift of God we'll cher - ish well, That ev - er

brought an an - gel bright. How great my joy! Great my joy!
hem a Child to - day. How great my joy! Great my joy!
shall re - deem us all. How great our joy! Great our joy!
joy our hearts shall fill. How great our joy! Great our joy!

Joy, joy, joy! Joy, joy, joy! Praise we the Lord in
Joy, joy, joy! Joy, joy, joy! Praise we the Lord in
Joy, joy, joy! Joy, joy, joy! Praise we the Lord in
Joy, joy, joy! Joy, joy, joy! Praise we the Lord in

heaven on high! Praise we the Lord in heaven on high!
heaven on high! Praise we the Lord in heaven on high!
heaven on high! Praise we the Lord in heaven on high!
heaven on high! Praise we the Lord in heaven on high!

HYMN TUNE: JUNGST

And there were in the same country shepherds abiding in the field, keeping watch over their flock by night. And, lo, the angel of the Lord came upon them, and the glory of the Lord shone round about them: and they were sore afraid. And the angel said unto them, Fear not: for, behold, I bring you good tidings of great joy, which shall be to all people. For unto you is born this day in the city of David a Saviour, which is Christ the Lord. And this shall be a sign unto you; Ye shall find the babe wrapped in swaddling clothes, lying in a manger. And suddenly there was with the angel a multitude of the heavenly host praising God, and saying. Glory to God in the highest, and on earth peace, good will toward men.

Luke 2:8-14

SHEPHERDS! SHAKE OFF YOUR DROWSY SLEEP

This carol may not be as familiar as many, but it is well worth the singer's time to learn it. The tune and text combine in a glorious song of expectation and joy as the shepherds receive the message of Jesus' birth.

Traditional French carol   Traditional French melody

1. Shep-herds! Shake off your drows - y sleep, Rise and leave your sil - ly
2. Hark! Ev - en now the bells ring round; Lis - ten to their mer - ry
3. Com-eth at length the age of peace, Strife and sor - row now shall
4. Shep-herds! Then up and quick a - way! Seek the Babe ere break of

sheep; An-gels from heaven a-round loud sing - ing, Tid ings of great joy are
sound! Hark! How the birds new songs are mak - ing, As if win - ter's chains were
cease; Proph-ets fore-told the won-drous sto - ry Of this heaven-born Prince of
day; He is the hope of ev - ery na - tion, All in him shall find sal-

REFRAIN

bring - ing. Shep-herds! The cho-rus come and swell! Sing Now - ell, O sing Now-ell!
break - ing.
glo - ry.
va - tion.

HYMN TUNE: BESANCON

And it came to pass, as the angels were gone away from them into heaven, the shepherds said one to another, Let us now go even unto Bethlehem, and see this thing which is come to pass, which the Lord hath made known unto us. And they came with haste, and found Mary, and Joseph, and the babe lying in a manger. And when they had seen it, they made known abroad the saying which was told them concerning this child. And all they that heard it wondered at those things which were told them by the shepherds. But Mary kept all these things, and pondered them in her heart.

Luke 2:15-19

WE THREE KINGS

John H. Hopkins, Jr.   John H. Hopkins, Jr.

1. We three kings of O - ri - ent are; Bear - ing
2. Born a King on Beth - le - hem's plain, Gold I
3. Frank - in - cense to of - fer have I; In - cense
4. Myrrh is mine: its bit - ter per - fume Breathes a
5. Glo - rious now be - hold him a - rise, King and

gifts we tra - verse a - far, Field and foun - tain,
bring to crown him a - gain, King for ev - er,
owns a De - i - ty nigh; Prayer and prais - ing
life of gath - er - ing gloom: Sor - rowing, sigh - ing,
God and sac - ri - fice; Al - le - lu - ia,

moor and moun - tain, Fol - low - ing yon - der star.
ceas - ing nev - er O - ver us all to reign.
all men rais - ing, Wor - ship him, God on high.
bleed - ing, dy - ing, Sealed in the stone - cold tomb.
Al - le - lu - ia! Sounds through the earth and skies.

Refrain

O star of won - der, star of night, Star with roy - al beau - ty bright.

West - ward lead - ing, still pro - ceed - ing, Guide us to thy per - fect light.

HYMN TUNE: KINGS OF ORIENT

Choruses
and
Prayers

B. Kimber

This section contains choruses and responses which may be used in intimate prayer group situations as well as the more formal confines of a large worship service. An effort has been made to include both traditional responses and service music in addition to many of the current choruses and songs which have proven so popular in contemporary settings of worship.

I WILL ENTER HIS GATES WITH THANKSGIVING

Joyfully

Composer Unknown

I will en-ter His gates with thanks-giv-ing in my heart, I will en-ter His courts with praise. I will say this is the day that the Lord has made, I will re-joice for He has made me glad. He has made me Glad, O He has made me glad, I will re-joice for He has made me glad. ——— He has made me Glad, O He has made me glad, I will re-joice for He has made me glad.

PRAISE ROUND

William Bay
Arr. L. Dean Bye

With movement

We praise, wor-ship and a-dore You, We laud, mag-ni-fy and bless You, Praise God, Praise God, Al - le - lu - ia,___ Praise God, Praise God Al -

Tambourine

1. le - lu - ia,___ We -le - lu - ia, Praise God!___

BLESS THE LORD, O MY SOUL

Psalm 103 : 1

Source Unknown

Bless the Lord, O my soul. Bless the Lord, O my soul and all that is with in me Bless His ho - ly name! A - men.

137

HOW GREAT IS OUR GOD

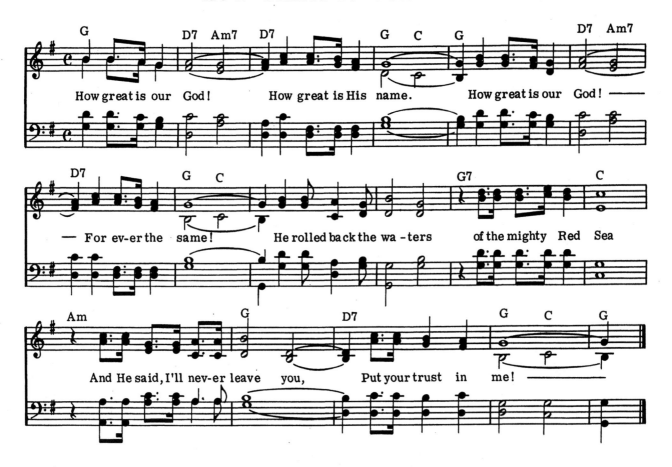

How great is our God! How great is His name. How great is our God! —— For ev-er the same! He rolled back the wa-ters of the mighty Red Sea And He said, I'll nev-er leave you, Put your trust in me! ——

RESPONSIVE ALLELUIA

Bill Bay

Al - le - lu - ia, Al - le - lu - ia, Al-le-lu - ia, Al-le-lu - ia!

GREAT IS THE LORD

Psalm 48

Robert Ewing

Great is the Lord and great-ly to be praised. In the
cit-y of our God In the moun-tain of His hol-i-ness
Beau-ti-ful for sit-u-a-tion, The joy of the whole earth
Is Mount Zi-on on the sides of the north the cit-y of the great King.

GOD IS SO GOOD

African

1. God is so good, God is so good, God is so good, He's so good to me.
2. He cares for me, He cares for me, He cares for me, He's so good to me.
3. I'll do His will, I'll do His will, I'll do His will, He's so good to me.
4. He loves me so, He loves me so, He loves me so, He's so good to me.
5. Je-sus is Lord, Je-sus is Lord, Je-sus is Lord, He's so good to me.

HE IS MY EVERYTHING

Composer Unknown

He is my ev-'ry-thing He is my all. He—is my ev-'ry-thing
He — is my all

both great and small. He He gave His life for me made ev-'ry-thing new
made

He He is my ev-'ry thing now how a-bout you. ——

HE'S ALL I NEED

Composer Unknown

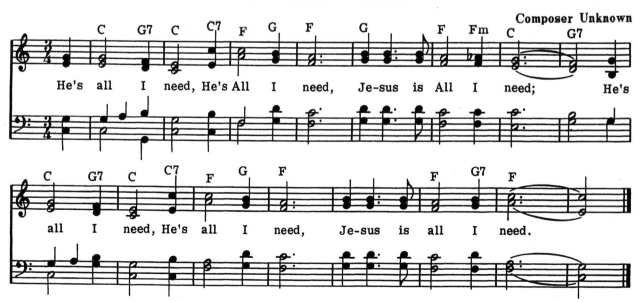

He's all I need, He's All I need, Je-sus is All I need; He's

all I need, He's all I need, Je-sus is all I need.

GATHER ROUND

Pamela C. Bye

Pamela C. Bye

And there is salvation in no one else, for there is no other name under heaven given among men by which we must be saved.

Acts 4:12

PRAISE GOD, FROM WHOM ALL BLESSINGS FLOW

Thomas Ken

Genevan Psalter

Praise God, from whom all blessings flow; Praise him, all creatures here below;

Praise him above, ye heavenly host; Praise Father, Son, and Holy Ghost. A-men.

WE GIVE THEE BUT THINE OWN

William How

Cantica Laudis, 1850

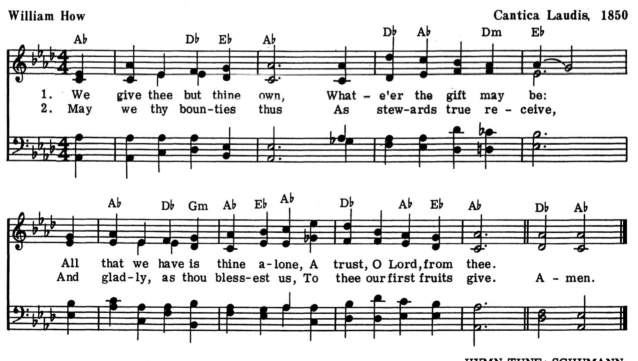

1. We give thee but thine own, What-e'er the gift may be:
2. May we thy boun-ties thus As stew-ards true re-ceive,

All that we have is thine a-lone, A trust, O Lord, from thee.
And glad-ly, as thou bless-est us, To thee our first fruits give. A-men.

HYMN TUNE: SCHUMANN

GLORY BE TO THE FATHER

Henry W. Greatorex

Glo-ry be to the Fa-ther, and to the Son, and to the Ho-ly Ghost; As it was in the be-gin-ning, is now, and ev-er shall be, world with-out end, A - men, A - men.

TWOFOLD AMEN

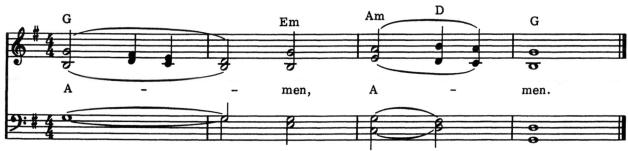

A - - men, A - men.

THREEFOLD AMEN

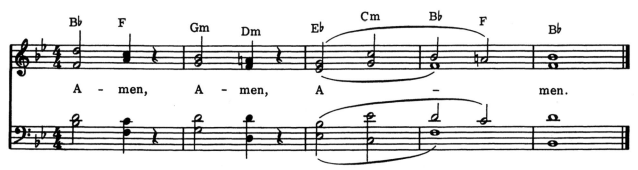

A - men, A - men, A - men.

HEAR OUR PRAYER, O LORD

Unknown

George Whelpton

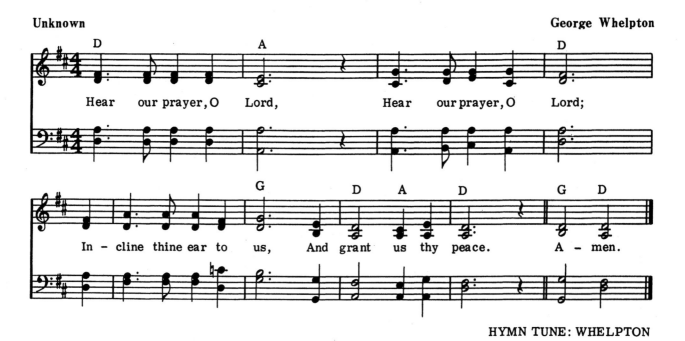

Hear our prayer, O Lord, Hear our prayer, O Lord; In-cline thine ear to us, And grant us thy peace. A-men.

HYMN TUNE: WHELPTON

SPIRIT OF THE LIVING GOD

Spir-it of the liv-ing God, fall fresh on me; Spir-it of the liv-ing God, fall fresh on me. Break me! Melt me! Mold me! Fill me! Spir-it of the liv-ing God, fall fresh on me. A-men.

WHISPER A PRAYER

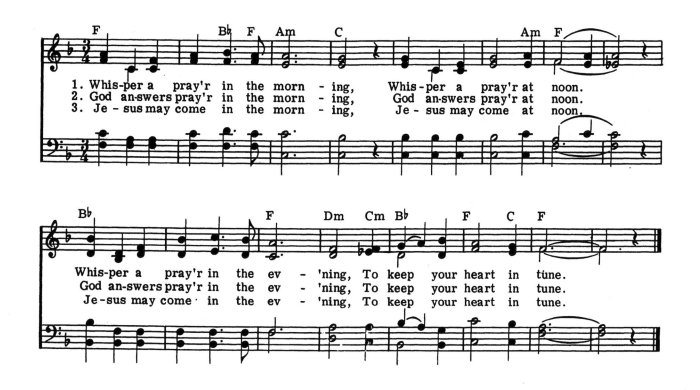

1. Whis-per a pray'r in the morn - ing, Whis-per a pray'r at noon.
2. God an-swers pray'r in the morn - ing, God an-swers pray'r at noon.
3. Je - sus may come in the morn - ing, Je - sus may come at noon.

Whis-per a pray'r in the ev - 'ning, To keep your heart in tune.
God an-swers pray'r in the ev - 'ning, To keep your heart in tune.
Je - sus may come in the ev - 'ning, To keep your heart in tune.

FATHER, WE THANK THEE

Rebecca J. Weston

D. Batchellor

1. Fa - ther, we thank Thee for the night, And for the pleas-ant morn-ing light,
2. Help us to do the things we should, To be to oth - ers kind and good;

For rest and food and lov-ing care, And all that makes the day so fair.
In all we do, in work or play, To grow more lov - ing ev - ery day.

GRANT US THY HOLY SPIRIT

Bill Bay

Bill Bay

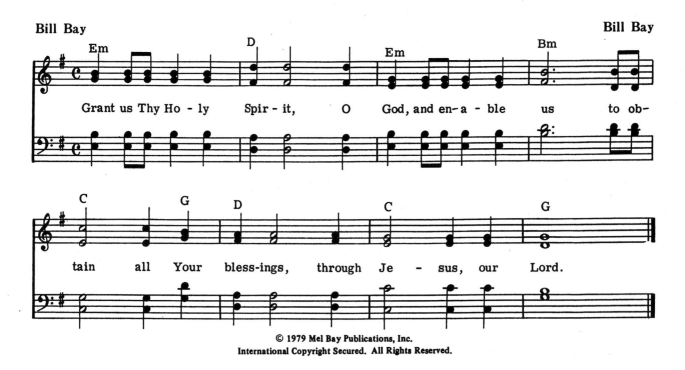

Grant us Thy Ho - ly Spir - it, O God, and en - a - ble us to ob-

tain all Your bless-ings, through Je - sus, our Lord.

GOD BE WITH YOU TILL WE MEET AGAIN

Jeremiah Rankin

William Tomer

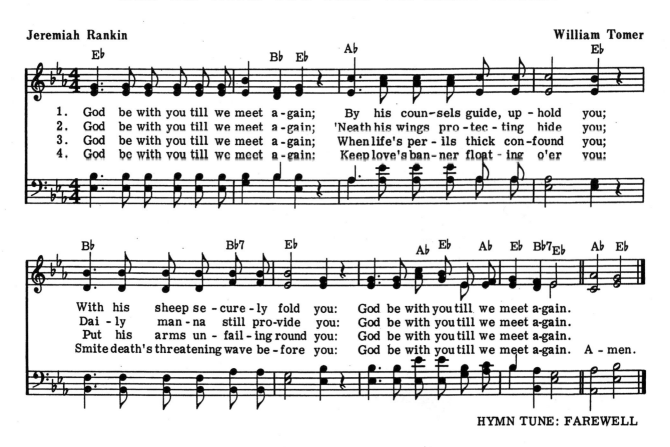

1. God be with you till we meet a - gain; By his coun-sels guide, up - hold you;
2. God be with you till we meet a - gain; 'Neath his wings pro-tec - ting hide you;
3. God be with you till we meet a - gain; When life's per - ils thick con-found you;
4. God be with you till we meet a - gain; Keep love's ban - ner float - ing o'er you;

With his sheep se - cure - ly fold you: God be with you till we meet a-gain.
Dai - ly man - na still pro-vide you: God be with you till we meet a-gain.
Put his arms un - fail - ing round you: God be with you till we meet a-gain.
Smite death's threatening wave be - fore you: God be with you till we meet a-gain. A - men.

HYMN TUNE: FAREWELL

146